Drama Structures

Drama Structures

A practical handbook for teachers

Cecily O'Neill and Alan Lambert

Hutchinson

London Melbourne Sydney Auckland Johannesburg

Hutchinson Education

An imprint of Century Hutchinson Ltd
62-65 Chandos Place, London WC2N 4NW

Century Hutchinson Australia Pty Ltd
PO Box 496, 16-22 Church Street, Hawthorn,
Victoria 3122, Australia

Century Hutchinson New Zealand Limited
PO Box 40-086, Glenfield, Auckland 10, New Zealand

Century Hutchinson South Africa (Pty) Limited
PO Box 337, Bergvlei 2012, South Africa

First published 1982
Reprinted 1983 (twice), 1984, 1985, 1987, 1988

© Cecily O'Neill and Alan Lambert 1982

Set in VIP Plantin by D. P. Media Limited, Hitchin, Hertfordshire

Printed and bound in Great Britain by Anchor Brendon Ltd, Tiptree, Essex

British Library Cataloguing in Publication Data
O'Neill, Cecily
  Drama structures.
  1. Drama – Study and teaching (Secondary)
  I. Title   II. Lambert, Alan
  792'.07'12   PN1701

ISBN 0 09 147811 1

Contents

Foreword

It seems to have become a tradition in publishing books on teaching drama to use a format that includes detailed illustrations from lessons observed. This book is part of that tradition, which began, I suspect, with Peter Slade's seminal *Child Drama* in which he described simple sequences of dramatic exercises conducted by himself and other teachers. What a long way we have come since the 1950s! What the readers are offered in this publication is a highly sophisticated account of complex teaching situations. These elaborate accounts are not included out of sheer love of complexity, but because the authors recognise that for teaching drama in this decade teachers need to adopt a more trenchant rationale and methodology: they must acquire a much wider range of techniques, including teacher-in-role and (so important) teacher-not-in-role; a stronger sense of what is essential to theatre form; a more sophisticated notion of drama for learning and, above all, a new respect for the 'content' or 'themes' for which drama can be the vehicle.

Thus the subject-matter is not drama *per se*, but any aspect of the curriculum which lends itself to dramatic structuring. This is not to be shrugged off as another attempt at an inter-disciplinary or integrated approach to the curriculum, for the reader will discover that the integrity of the basic concepts of any particular discipline remains intact. This book should therefore be useful to all teachers, for specialists in other fields may identify within its pages approaches to their own subjects which could be adapted to their own teaching styles.

One of the problems for drama teachers in the past has been that text books giving practical help have tended to limit their illustrations to accounts of single lessons. One of the strengths of this text is that its authors have undertaken to describe, step by step, whole projects which may cover several week's work.

But the greatest achievement of the book is the way it sets out *to teach*. The reader is not only able to follow what happened in someone else's teaching, he or she is presented at critical points with a close analysis of the choices open to the teacher concerned. From this the reader is guided into a discussion of principles behind these choices and shown how, under different circumstances (perhaps the reader's own teaching context) alternative routes would seem to be more appropriate. It is this sharing of principles, this going beyond the attraction and limitation of a particular illustration that places this book in the forefront of teachers' manuals to date.

Gavin Bolton
University of Durham
February 1982

Acknowledgements

We wish to acknowledge our debt to Gavin Bolton and Dorothy Heathcote who remain a continual source of inspiration.

For the many opportunities we have had to try out our ideas in London schools and for a great deal of support and encouragement, we would like to thank the ILEA Drama Inspectorate, our colleagues in the drama advisory service, and all the ILEA pupils and teachers with whom we have worked, particularly Gill Walker and Elyse Dodgson.

For permission to reproduce the following photographs the authors and publisher would like to thank:

Denver Public Library, Western History Department, 1357 Broadway, Denver, Colorado 80203 – page 32

Piccadilly Advice Centre, 9 Archer Street, London W1 – page 60

Macdonald Educational, Maxwell House, 74 Worship Street, London EC2A 2EN – page 82

Barnardo's, Tanners Lane, Barkingside, Ilford, Essex IG6 1QG – page 106

Preface

Our aim in this book is to help teachers to develop the kinds of flexible framework which will support their work in the drama lesson. In secondary schools, drama can often become isolated from the rest of the school curriculum and from the areas of significant content which are available to teachers in other subject areas. When this happens, drama may become superficial and fragmented. Because of external pressures of time and space, the teacher may be forced to rely too heavily on games and exercises, or may emphasize theatre skills which are practised externally to any exploration or development of meaning.

We feel that what is lacking is not access to drama 'ideas', which are provided in many different handbooks, but suggestions for the kinds of structure which will help teachers in extending these ideas and in working in greater depth with their pupils. If pupils are to grasp concepts, understand complex issues, solve problems and work creatively and co-operatively in drama, they will be helped by a clearly established context and a strong but flexible framework to support and extend the meaning of the work.

The first part of this book, 'Drama in Schools', offers a simple theoretical basis for the work which follows, and considers the kinds of learning which drama can promote. All the practical examples given in this section are taken from the structures described later in the book. We hope that this section will assist teachers in analysing and refining their own view of drama in education.

In Part 2, 'The Structures', we describe four structures for drama in considerable detail. As well as outlining the kinds of dramatic activity which might take place, we consider the teaching points which arise from each activity.

The third section of the book, 'Teaching Drama', provides checklists which are designed to help teachers in planning, operating and evaluating their own drama lessons, and which may lead them towards an understanding of the elements which promote effective drama teaching.

In the final part of the book, 'Structures for Development', we hope that the series of lessons we describe will encourage teachers to develop their own approaches to drama and will enable them to use ideas and strategies from elsewhere in the book to extend their own work in fruitful and appropriate directions.

Throughout, we see the drama teacher as central to the activity of the lesson. It is the teacher, working with the pupils within the drama, who will build on the pupils' ideas and make a bridge for them between their own experience of the world and the meaning of the drama, so that both insight and understanding arise from the activity. Although the structures described in this book suggest clear directions for the drama, the work will only be fully successful when teachers, within the kind of security which these structures seek to provide, accept the ideas brought to the work by the pupils, recognize the demands of the material and find new directions of their own. Ideally, the suggested structures will be stepping-off points for each group's own exploration and development, rather than exact 'recipes' which must be adhered to at all costs.

No book can replace a teacher. If drama is successful it will be because of the skills teachers use to motivate their pupils, to build on their contributions, and select, focus and pace the different activities in the lesson. This book will have achieved its purpose when teachers are sufficiently confident to dispense with the suggestions it provides and develop their own structures for exploration in drama. Finally, it is only through the teacher's own commitment to and involvement in the work that drama will realize its full potential as a medium for learning.

Part 1   *Drama in Schools*

What is drama?

Drama in education is a mode of learning. Through the pupils' active identification with imagined roles and situations in drama, they can learn to explore issues, events and relationships.

In drama, children draw on their knowledge and experience of the real world in order to create a make-believe world. So, in tackling a theme like 'The Way West' (Structure 1) they will call on their own experience of travelling or leaving home, as well as on knowledge about wagon trains and the Wild West, gained from books, films or television. At first the make-believe may be superficial and action-oriented, but with the teacher's guidance and intervention it should be possible for the work to grow in depth. In creating and reflecting on this make-believe world pupils can come to understand themselves and the real world in which they live.

In order to engage in dramatic activity pupils do not need sophisticated theatre skills. However, they must be willing to:
Make-believe with regard to objects
For example:

> A table-top can become a wagon or a raft. (Structure 1)
> A circle of chairs may represent a starship. (Structure 13)
> Cupped hands may contain a precious object. (Structure 4)

Make-believe with regard to actions and situations
For example:

> Creeping across the school hall may be the means of escaping from the workhouse. (Structure 4)
> A group sitting huddled on the floor may be steerage passengers on board an emigrant ship. (Structure 11)
> Stealing a bunch of keys may represent a test of stealth and cunning for the warriors. (Structure 12)

Adopt a role
For example:

Settlers who seek a new life in Oregon. (Structure 1)
Poor children living on the streets of London. (Structure 4)
Teenagers who have left home. (Structure 2)

Maintain the make-believe verbally
For example:

Describing the doorway in which they spent the night. (Structure 4)
Presenting the facts about child labour to the committee for reform.
(Structure 4)
Discussing the problems to be faced on the voyage to the New World.
(Structure 11)
Telling one of the rumours about the Haunted house. (Structure 7)

Interact with the rest of the group
For example:

Agreeing to join the crew of the starship. (Structure 13)
Choosing a leader for the community. (Structure 3)
Making a group decision about the meeting with the Indians. (Structure 1)
Showing a scene from the life of the workhouse. (Structure 4)
Teaching a skill to a friend. (Structure 3)

Most pupils will have developed these essential skills through dramatic play. At secondary-school level they may need to be encouraged to discover them again in a new context. Some children may never have experienced play of this kind and may be unwilling or unable to 'pretend'. Drama is unlikely to develop successfully unless the participants are prepared to make-believe in the ways listed above, to share their make-believe with others by working together, and to maintain and extend their make-believe through appropriate action, role and language.

The participants must be able to understand and accept the 'rules of the game' as they would if they were playing together. Whatever the age of the pupils, the 'rules of the game' in drama remain the same. These 'rules' will not necessarily be formulated in advance, but the participants must allow themselves to be bound by the constraints of the structure in which they are working. For example, the inmates of the workhouse must accept the harsh conditions unless they can find appropriate ways of altering them (Structure 3). Only actions which fit the rules of behaviour will be acceptable in the make-believe. Both teacher and class are likely to recognize very readily which kinds of language and behaviour are inappropriate and destructive. For the drama process to be meaningful and satisfying, both personally and educationally, the participants must selectively apply their relevant knowledge and experience of the real world to fit the demands of the make-believe roles and situations. When they do, they will be working with belief, commitment and integrity.

DRAMA AND THE GROUP

Drama is essentially social and involves contact, communication and the negotiation of meaning. The group nature of the work will impose certain pressures on the participants but will also bring considerable rewards.

Co-operative activity is rare in our schools. Too often, pupils are trained to work as individuals and to be both competitive and possessive about their achievements. Any kind of sharing may be actively discouraged. Drama, on the other hand, works from the strength of the group. It draws on a common stock of experiences and in turn enriches the minds and feelings of individuals within the group.

The meaning of the drama is built up from the contributions of individuals, and, if the work is to develop, these contributions must be monitored, understood, accepted and responded to by the rest of the group. The group here means the whole class unit, including the teacher. As Dewey points out, it is absurd to exclude the teacher from membership of the group.

In drama, the representation of experience which each individual offers to the group is subject to the scrutiny of the rest. What is offered may be modified by others who in turn must modify their own contributions. Each person's addition to the make-believe is subject to a kind of reality test by the rest of the group. The ability of the group to build on each other's contributions and to respond appropriately will increase with practice in the process, and will be accompanied by a growing confidence in handling unexpected or unpredictable elements which arise.

Within the safe framework of the make-believe, individuals can see their ideas and suggestions accepted and used by the group. They can learn how to influence others; how to marshal effective arguments and present them appropriately; how to put themselves in other people's shoes. They can try out roles and receive immediate feedback. The group can become a powerful source of creative ideas and effective criticism.

DRAMA AND LEARNING

The most significant kind of learning which is attributable to experience in drama is a growth in the pupils' understanding about human behaviour, themselves and the world they live in. This growth of understanding, which will involve changes in customary ways of thinking and feeling, is likely to be the primary aim of drama teaching. A secondary aim will be an increased competence in using the drama form and satisfaction from working within it.

Theatre skills are not necessary before a group engages in drama, but working in drama is likely to develop and enhance those skills. Both drama and theatre skills will grow inside the work. A drama skill such as the successful adoption of a role – a poor child meeting a philanthropic lady (Structure 4) – will grow from being *in* the situation. It need not be practised outside the drama. A theatre skill – showing in movement the most difficult stage of the journey across the plains (Structure 1) – will also develop from the motivation and significance provided by the context of the drama.

As well as these long-term aims, the drama teacher is likely to have particular objectives for each lesson, directly related to the needs of the class. These may include:

Learning which arises from the content of the lesson
For example:

A knowledge of the facts about poverty, city life and child labour in Victorian times. (Structure 4)
A realization of the degree of exploitation and injustice suffered by the Indians. (Structure 1)
A grasp of the factors which led to the European emigrations of the nineteenth century. (Structure 11)

Social learning
For example:

Increased social competence and confidence.
The ability to work purposefully with others.
Willingness to accept and respect the ideas of others and to build on them.
Willingness to accept responsibility.
The opportunity to escape from an existing self-image or 'role' in the group – clown, trouble-maker, outsider.

Skills
For example:

Increased skill in language use.
Confidence and skill in movement.
The ability to operate successfully in a variety of roles.
The ability to communicate ideas effectively to others.
The ability to shape and select material for performance.

These areas of learning are to some degree demonstrable and measurable. It ought to be possible for teachers to observe and assess growth in pupils in all of these areas.

Intrinsic learning
The primary aim of drama teaching – a growth or change in understanding – is more difficult to demonstrate and assess. It is unlikely to be achieved unless there is both motivation and self-discipline and the participants are working with integrity of feeling and thought. In the drama, decisions must be honoured, consequences faced and responsibility accepted. Reflection will play an important part in this kind of learning. Where the drama teacher's primary aim is achieved, the participants will grow in insight and understanding, they will make discoveries about attitudes and implications, and they will grasp truths to do with human behaviour and its consequences. Through the drama process it may become possible for them to make sense of their experience in the world and begin to organize it into the unity, significance and coherence of art.

Drama and the curriculum

Drama has considerable potential as a process with wide educational implications within the school curriculum. It is an activity which can promote:

Enquiry

> What factors caused the emigrants to leave for the New World? (Structure 11)
> What conditions do the child labourers have to endure? (Structure 4)
> What is the true history of the haunted house? (Structure 7)
> Why did this person become a criminal? (Structure 8)
> How did the disaster occur which rendered the land uninhabitable? (Structure 9)

Critical and constructive thought

> Is it right that the family at the Big House are rich, while the chimney-sweeps sleep on straw? (Structure 4)
> How should the hostel for young homeless people be organized? (Structure 2)
> How are the facts of Macbeth's reign to be presented so that tyranny will never recur? (Structure 14)
> How can the advertising campaign be tailored to reach its target? (Structure 15)

Problem-solving

> Is it possible to demonstrate to the Alien that men are intelligent? (Structure 13)

What will be the most effective means of administering charity? (Structure 4)
How can the Indians be persuaded to allow the settlers through their territory? (Structure 1)
What preparations should be made if the community is to survive the winter? (Structure 3)

Skills of comparison, interpretation, judgement and discrimination

Who is really to blame for the accident to the chimney-sweep? (Structure 4)
What are the implications of the clues found by the detectives? Which are relevant and which should be ignored? (Structure 6)
What is the significance of the differences in the appearance of the child's bedroom? (Structure 5)
What is the meaning of the ritual performed by the primitive tribe? (Structure 3)
Can the visitor to the workhouse be trusted? (Structure 4)
Is it possible to negotiate peace terms with the Indians? (Structure 1)

Further learning and research

What reforms were carried out in nineteenth-century child labour? (Structure 4)
Did the white men keep their treaties with the Indians? (Structure 1)
Does the law treat men and women differently? (Structure 13)
What provision is made for homeless young people in London today? (Structure 2)
What influence did Lady Macbeth have on her husband's behaviour? (Structure 14)

In the primary school it is potentially easier for drama to act as an integrating force in the curriculum and for teachers to draw on different subject areas in order to create a wide range of learning outcomes from the drama. In secondary schools, in spite of the rigid framework of the timetable, there is increasing recognition of the value of drama strategies in English, humanities, social studies and moral education, and of the effectiveness of these practical strategies in motivating, stimulating and challenging pupils. Any view of drama which restricts it to a forty-minute hall or studio activity is limiting its potential as a learning medium.

In case we seem to be advocating that drama should be regarded as a handmaid in the teaching of other subjects, it is important to realize that when drama is used in other curriculum areas it is not necessarily a mere servicing agent. There will be a two-way process taking place. Other subject areas will provide drama with serious and worthwhile content and, in many cases, a powerful context for the make-believe, while drama strategies will enliven and illuminate these areas of the curriculum. The involvement of drama in these other areas will give significance to the activity, strengthen the commitment and belief of the pupils, and increase their willingness to work seriously and constructively. As Tom Stabler points out in *Drama in Primary Schools*, the link between drama and other curricular outcomes can be dynamic and not merely a passive means to convenient follow-up activities.

If drama is to be used as a medium for learning in specific areas of the curriculum, it is important to be clear about the kinds of learning that pupils are expected to achieve. The teacher must be satisfied that drama will be the most appropriate means of promoting this kind of learning. If the work involves an understanding of human experience in particular circumstances, the exploration of attitudes and opinions, or the representation of abstract concepts in concrete form, then drama will be an appropriate way of working.

HISTORY

Many of the themes used as a basis for the structures in this book are historical and history is one of the subjects which seem an obvious choice for the inclusion of drama strategies. But many teachers will discern problems in this way of working. In the teaching of history there is a need for authenticated realities, and drama is to do with imagined realities. The purpose of using drama strategies is not to transmit historical facts but is an attempt to illuminate those facts.

In using an historical basis for their drama, pupils face the challenge of creating an alternative and convincing world while maintaining points of comparison with the real world, so that the two can be fruitfully related. The emphasis will be on discovery rather than on mere implementation of factual knowledge. Pupils will be aware that their drama world is an imaginative product to which they apply factual knowledge in order to sustain dramatic credibility. One of the responsibilities of the drama teacher will be to reinforce this awareness.

Although the primary purpose of using drama strategies will not be to teach facts, this may be one of the outcomes of the work. True historical awareness requires a sensitivity to the flow and tensions of human events of the past. The study of history has been described as a journey in feeling and in thought through a succession of contingencies, into the time in which we live. Drama can help our pupils to maintain a sense of significant continuity with the past and assist them in functioning in a more coherent present. It will be a step in the process of maturity when people, concepts and events are no longer regarded as fixed and static, but are seen to alter and evolve in response to circumstance. There will be fresh insight into the nature of history and the work of the historian when enquiry, speculation and interpretation are recognized as part of the process of understanding the past. Drama connects us with the past and makes it available, while affirming human values which transcend the concepts of past and present.

LANGUAGE

One of the most positive contributions which drama makes to the curriculum is that it provides a facilitating atmosphere for many kinds of language use. Language is the cornerstone of the drama process and the means through which the drama is realized. Whenever any kind of active role-play takes place, language is directly and necessarily involved. Drama can provide a powerful motivation to speech, and this speech does not occur in isolation but is embedded in context and situation where it has a crucial organizing function.

The language of both teacher and pupil can:

Create and control the situation

> 'Here is the key to the haunted house. Who will have the courage to use it?' (Structure 7)
> 'The monster Grendel has attacked again. He must be destroyed.' (Structure 12)

Regulate the activity

> 'We have been on this trail before. Follow us and we can show you the only place where it is safe to cross the river.' (Structure 1)
> 'Which of the warriors is prepared to undergo the trial of strength?' (Structure 12)

Define the roles

> 'We have lived in the workhouse for many years. We can tell you the injustices we have suffered.' (Structure 4)
> 'I can speak for the people of my tribe. We do not wish the white men to enter our territory.' (Structure 1)

Bind the group together

> 'We must decide how we will welcome the strangers.' (Structure 3)
> 'How can we discover the truth of what has happened here?' (Structure 6)

The approaches in this book include activities which seek to extend and enhance the language of individuals in the group through the active and collective nature of the work. The need to deliberate, negotiate, implement decisions and assess consequences will be an essential part of the process and will inevitably make demands on pupils' language resources.

Drama makes it possible for both teachers and pupils to escape from the more familiar patterns of language interaction which exist in the classroom and offers them both a new range of possibilities. The pupils need no longer be dominated by the teacher's language but can use it as a sounding-board for their own developing capacities. In particular, role challenge for both teacher and pupil is likely to release qualities of language not previously available or recognized, and the approaches described in this book seek to exploit this challenge. The teacher speaking as Warden of the workhouse may sound very much like 'teacher', but in role as a parent whose child has left home he or she may have to find a different kind of language. The teacher's search for appropriate registers for the different roles which may be adopted in the drama will encourage pupils to find appropriate roles and language styles for themselves. The teacher's language should be encouraging, exploratory and available, leading pupils to involve themselves actively in the make-believe and the talk which arises from it.

It should be possible for the teacher to appraise the language capacities of individual pupils within the drama and to judge whether they are able to handle the following crucial categories of language effectively:

Describing past experiences, both real and imaginary

> Remembering a time when they were lost or lonely. (Structure 2)
> Describing the escape from the workhouse. (Structure 4)
> Recalling the land they have left behind for ever. (Structure 11)

Instructing and explaining

> Teaching the members of the expedition the techniques of hunting. (Structure 3)
> Explaining the best way of crossing the river. (Structure 1)
> Presenting the evidence to the committee for reform. (Structure 4)

Logical reasoning, convincing, persuading

> Listing possible reasons for the disappearance of the missing girl. (Structure 6)
> Apportioning blame for the chimney-sweep's accident. (Structure 4)
> Asking a rich person for charity. (Structure 4)
> Persuading the family to leave for the New World. (Structure 11)

Planning, predicting, deciding

> Choosing the best means of helping London's homeless children. (Structure 4)
> Preparing for a night in the haunted house. (Structure 7)
> Anticipating what life will be like in Oregon. (Structure 1)
> Considering the consequences of a battle with the settlers. (Structure 1)
> Deciding what to do about the baby which has been found. (Structure 3)

As pupils develop competence in using language, they also learn basic attitudes to the world around them, to the people and events within it, and to learning itself. Teachers who are concerned to create opportunities for language use within the drama must be prepared to:

Create an atmosphere where talk is the norm and in which pupils' contributions are valued.

Support, extend and if necessary elaborate on what is offered.

Press for extension of inadequate contributions without rejecting what pupils have offered.

Work appropriately in role, finding styles which help to model appropriate language for the class.

Seek further information from the class and offer insights and information without burdening the class with the teacher's own knowledge.

Remodel the language which has been received if it is incorrect or inappropriate, without seeming to correct or reject it.

Use non-verbal activities to enrich the phases of the lesson in which talk occurs.

Find reading and writing tasks which arise from the drama and which will deepen the pupils' understanding.

As Tom Stabler points out, drama offers the possibility of a synthesis between language, feeling and thought, which can enrich the individual's inner world and increase his or her awareness and understanding of the outer world, as well as his or her competence and confidence in operating within it. It would be prodigal of the drama teacher to neglect such a possibility.

Whatever subject is approached through drama, the kinds of learning which may arise will not primarily derive from inputs of new information by the teacher. Pupils will have to make their own relationships with the topic and articulate their own personal responses within the drama. As well as the material which is to be illuminated through drama strategies, the teacher will be working with what the pupils already know and think and feel – the material which is already in their heads and which has come to them from their experience in the world. Since a large proportion of the content of the lesson will be contributed by the pupils, it will be unpredictable. So will the learning which may result. The kinds of knowledge and understanding which pupils may acquire from the drama lesson will not always be easy to predict or specify. It may be impossible for the teacher to set this learning out as a series of propositions or outcomes. But these understandings will be displayed by being brought to bear on particular situations in life, or on imagined situations in the drama.

Teachers who use drama must accept that in this kind of approach knowledge is not given but made. Because it is an aesthetic medium the lesson will contain more than can be stated discursively and a diverse range of learning processes, both cognitive and affective, will be included. Outcomes will be unpredictable.

The validity of the knowledge and experience which pupils already possess will be recognized and included in the work.

But for the teacher who undertakes this way of working the rewards are likely to be considerable. Motivation and understanding will be strengthened, language use extended, flexibility of mind encouraged, concepts tested, and opportunities created for creative thinking and problem-solving.

The drama teacher

The drama teacher, like the teacher of any other subject, must accept responsibility for what takes place during the lesson. In any classroom, it will be the teacher who selects the activity, communicates knowledge, encourages the growth of skills and enforces standards of behaviour. What is learnt in the lesson will be the result of choices made by the teacher, whether conscious or unconscious, and these will depend on such factors as underlying philosophy, and attitudes to pupils and the subject which is being taught.

The drama teacher's function, in the structures which follow, is not primarily to instruct pupils or to pass on any body of knowledge. The teacher is seen as attempting to create potential areas of learning in which pupils can participate. If pupils are to be encouraged to accept a greater degree of responsibility for their own learning it may be necessary for teachers to re-examine their attitudes and relationships in the classroom. They may need to alter their teaching style gradually, so that pupils can adapt to new approaches, and they will no longer be able to adopt the familiar teacher stance of being the 'one who knows'. They must be prepared to build on the knowledge and experience which pupils bring with them to the work, and they must value their pupils' contributions to the lesson more than their own. To some extent, they must be prepared to put themselves in their pupils' hands while retaining the functions, duties and responsibilities of the teacher.

As far as the drama lesson is concerned, the teacher's functions, duties and responsibilities will include the following:

Setting up the kinds of structures which allow for the spontaneity of the pupils but which are likely to engage them in purposeful learning.
Selecting themes and topics which will interest and motivate the group.
Choosing activities which are within the competence of the group but which will stretch their developing capacities.
Eliciting creative responses from the group.
Focusing the thinking of the group and challenging superficial responses.
Identifying and supporting contributions which have potential for learning.
Finding structures which expose pupils to issues in the doing of them.
Encouraging the group to explore what they don't know rather than re-enact what they *do* know.

Pacing the growth of the work so that integrity and depth of thinking and feeling are encouraged to develop.
Remaining flexible in teaching intentions.
Going beyond original planning in pursuit of learning opportunities.
Observing which attitudes and tendencies are being encouraged, and judging which are likely to lead to growth and which are detrimental.
Finding satisfying form for pupils' ideas and insights.
Reinforcing the learning which the group may achieve and co-ordinating their achievements.
Encouraging reflection and evaluation.

The structures and approaches described in this book assume that the teacher has an essential function in the drama process. For too long the drama teacher has been seen as operating outside the creative process, as facilitator for the creativity of the pupils, with a function restricted to that of provider of a stimulus or commentator on an end-product. But, left to themselves, pupils are likely to work only at a superficial level in which they repeat or re-enact their existing insights. If teachers are part of the creative process from the beginning of the work, it is more likely that their structuring and intervention will lead to fresh understanding and insight for their pupils. By becoming part of the drama process, the teacher can share in the experience, give it significance, and influence and control the work from within. In the structures which follow the teacher's function as part of the process is thoroughly explored, particularly in the section on 'Working in role'.

Modes of dramatic activity

The structures which follow include a number of different modes of dramatic activity:
Exercise
Dramatic playing
Theatre   *
   These modes will fulfil a variety of purposes and will require different kinds of classroom organization. Each of these dramatic activities will be part of an overall framework and, if the appropriate activity has been selected, should enrich the developing meaning of the work. By engaging in a variety of dramatic modes, the participants should develop their drama skills and become familiar with and adept at using the medium of drama. Different activities may allow for the practice of particular drama skills. However, practice of these skills does not

*These categories are taken from Gavin Bolton's *Towards a Theory of Drama in Education*, where they are discussed in greater detail.

occur in isolation but within a chosen context, and as an integral part of the dramatic process.

EXERCISE

Examples from the structures:

> A survivor of the last great battle with the white people tells a young member of the tribe what happened. (Structure 1)
> A chimney-sweep describes to a friend an object which he has noticed in the big house. (Structure 4)
> The settlers sing around the camp-fire to keep up their courage. (Structure 1)
> The warriors demonstrate their stealth and courage by stealing the keys. (Structure 12)
> A villager tells the legends of the haunted house to a stranger in the pub. (Structure 7)
> The settlers list what they will take with them in their wagons. (Structure 1)
> The members of the expedition demonstrate their skills to each other. (Structure 3)
> The teenage suspects are questioned by the police. (Structure 8)

These activities are likely to be brief in duration, and may include a specific task or goal. They will be introduced by the teacher, whose instructions should be clear and concise.

The exercise form may present difficulties for some classes, particularly at an early stage in the work. These difficulties may include:

> The lack of sufficient social or dramatic skills to maintain the make-believe for each other and to complete the task.
> An inability to maintain appropriate language or role.
> A tendency to work in stereotype and to avoid challenge or serious engagement with the task.

The experience may be uneven in quality, depending on the skill and commitment of the participants.
It may be difficult for the teacher to get sufficient feedback from the pairs or the groups to know what the experience has been for them.

DRAMATIC PLAYING

Examples from the structures:

> Exploring the Lost Valley. (Structure 3)
> A day in the life of the settlers. (Structure 1)

> On board the emigrant ship. (Structure 11)
> Caring for the injured after the disaster. (Structure 9)
> The starship takes off. (Structure 13)
> Life in the workhouse. (Structure 4)

This kind of dramatic activity is usually spontaneous and open-ended in form. The responsibility for maintaining the make-believe and developing the action rests entirely with the group and, although the teacher may support what the class is doing, intervention may not be appropriate. There will be times when it is important for the class to operate in this way. Because they have been given the opportunity to 'play', the dramatic situation may come alive for the pupils and they may begin to believe in and commit themselves to the activity. It may be necessary for them to go through this phase before being able to accept challenge in the drama. It is possible that themes which are important to the class may emerge from this kind of work.

The problems it presents include the following:

> The level of thinking is often shallow and the structure rambling.
> It may be difficult for the teacher to find a way into the experience.
> The teacher may find it difficult to move the class from this level of working so that they can be challenged within the experience.
> Some classes may be used to working in this way and may resent being denied the freedom it offers them.
> The energy level of the class may be high but it may be impossible to harness this energy other than in physical action.
> Individual experiences which occur may be difficult to include in the overall framework.
> If the class is working in this way in small groups, it may be difficult to determine what the experience has been for different groups.
> Because work in this mode lacks a central focus, the drama may be dissipated and a number of different and conflicting themes may emerge.
> This absence of a clear focus for the work and the lack of dramatic tension which is likely to result may mean that the experience becomes frustrating and unsatisfying for the group.

THEATRE

Examples from the structures:

> Show the circumstances which caused the emigrants to leave their homes. (Structure 11)
> Re-enact the events of the night when the girl disappeared. (Structure 6)

> Prepare a series of tableaux to show life in the workhouse. (Structure 4)
> Prepare a ritual to celebrate success in hunting. (Structure 3)
> Show some of the strange happenings in the haunted house. (Structure 7)
> Re-create the last battle between settlers and Indians. (Structure 1)

This kind of activity can make considerable demands on the participants, for, in addition to the social skills needed to enable each pupil to function effectively as a member of a group, they will also be required to exercise a wide range of drama skills. To operate successfully in this mode pupils must be able to:

> Select a suitable dramatic focus for their work.
> Choose appropriate characters, settings, incident, action and dialogue.
> Use objects, furniture and costume where necessary, in order to add significant detail.
> Employ technical skills relating to performance, including audibility, gesture, variation of pace and delivery.
> Find the most economical means of expression in order to create an effective piece of theatre.
> Practise, revise and reshape the work.
> Comment on their own and others' efforts in a positive manner.
> Take a share in the responsibilities of performance.
> Accept and make use of the critical comment of observers.

Too often this kind of activity can result in a superficial playing out of events, lacking in seriousness and sometimes accompanied by a certain degree of showing off. This is particularly likely to happen when groups are aiming at the kind of naturalism which is beyond their present skills. The teacher should be able to give the work a stronger sense of purpose and motivation by using it for specific objectives within an established drama context. It can be used to:

Provide a starting-point for enquiry
Groups prepare a short scene encapsulating their particular viewpoint on a chosen theme or topic, for example emigrants, young offenders, a woman's place. (Structures 11, 8, 10)
  The ideas which are expressed in dramatic form will give the teacher some indication of the pupils' interest in the material and their existing grasp of the theme.

Provide evidence and information
Various aspects of a theme, life-style, or problem can be illustrated in a number of different scenes in order to build up a fuller picture of a particular way of life, for example, the differences between rich and poor in Victorian times. (Structure 4)

Present an alternative reconstruction of events
Each group' shows a different version of the circumstances leading up to a situation in which events are open to interpretation, for example what exactly happened when the child's bedroom was wrecked? (Structure 5)

Present alternative courses of action
Groups illustrate a suitable solution to a problem with which they are concerned, for example different versions of how the runaways can be reconciled with their parents. (Structure 4)

Provide a means of reflection
Each group prepares a short scene or series of scenes summing up the most significant areas of their work on a particular theme, for example the struggle of women for the vote. (Structure 10)
A variety of styles and dramatic forms can be used, including dance drama, mime, tableaux and melodrama.

SMALL-GROUP WORK

Small-group work, in whatever mode, is likely to present a variety of problems. These will include:

Difficulties of control for the teacher, because several groups are working at the same time.
The task of monitoring the progress of each group and intervening effectively may be made almost impossible since the teacher is on the outside of the work.
In the exercise and theatre modes in particular, pupils may be demonstrating their existing understanding rather than learning anything new or experiencing any growth of insight.
The teacher may find it difficult to assist pupils to deepen their work and to move away from cliché, stereotype, and superficial showing-off.
Problems of leadership may emerge, and groups may rely on one or two people to provide ideas and organize the work.
In small-group work, real relationships within the class may interfere with the make-believe relationships which are being established in the drama.
There may be problems of timing and feedback. Groups may differ in the length of time they need to prepare and show their work. It may be impossible within the lesson for each group to prepare and show its work, and for the teacher and the rest of the class to comment usefully on what has been presented.

However, there are a number of advantages to be gained from small-group work that is introduced as part of an overall dramatic context, so that what is attempted is not fragmented or irrelevant.

A topic can be examined on a scale which would otherwise be impossible.

The activities of the groups can be seen to complement each other, since they are part of the same context.

Demands will be made on pupils to accept considerable responsibility. Although individual participation and responsibility may be increased, pupils are also part of an undertaking shared by the whole class.

Pupils are presented with the challenge of completing a task.

The groups' response to the task will give a clear indication of the level of their thinking and their emotional and intellectual grasp of the topic.

Changes in the pattern of work will show up strengths and weaknesses in the competence of pupils, and their commitment to and understanding of the theme.

The pupils' capacity to investigate material and extract relevant and significant detail should be increased.

The groups may begin to acquire a command of dramatic form.

If a teacher is setting up small-group work in any mode there are a number of considerations which must be taken into account.

The work should serve a purpose within the overall structure, whether it is designed to provide more information, deepen the thinking or feeling, extend the skills of the participants, or provide a change of pace or activity.

The task must be made clear, and should be within the social and dramatic competence of the class.

Appropriate sized groups should be established.

Pupils should be encouraged to work with different partners and outside their own friendship groups.

The teacher should be available to give guidance and supervision to each group.

There must be enough time for groups to complete their tasks or reach their goals, and, where appropriate, share their work with the rest of the class.

WHOLE-GROUP DRAMA

Although exercise, dramatic playing and theatre will all contribute to the value of the experience, it is likely that the most valuable kinds of learning will take place when the group is working as a whole. It is impossible to guarantee that drama which has depth and integrity will occur, but it is at points in the structure when the class is working spontaneously together and when the teacher is part of the process that participants are most likely to question, accept challenges, make decisions, realize implications, go beyond stereotypes and alter their perspectives. If the class is working with belief, commitment and integrity the pupils may even achieve the kind of change in understanding which is at the heart of educational drama.

Such points in the following structures might include:

The trial of the young thieves. (Structures 4 and 8)

The meeting of the Indians with a white man. (Structure 1)

The finding of the baby from the primitive tribe. (Structure 3)

The encounter between the crew of the starship and the Alien. (Structure 13)

The moment when the Ladies' Guild are asked to support the Suffragettes. (Structure 10)

It is also at these points in the structure that the work is most likely to take a new direction. If a particular class has become deeply involved in a crisis point in the drama it may become obvious to the teacher that it will be irrelevant to proceed in the direction suggested by the structure. The teacher must be prepared to try to identify what the experience has been for the class and attempt to determine what the next step in the drama should be. The teacher will not be thinking in terms of plot – 'what happens next' – but will be searching for a means of extending the learning for the group, and making the experience more significant for them.

Although it may be tempting for the teacher to think in terms of narrative development, drama does not work in the same way as story. It is not the simple unfolding of a sequence of events, although the necessity of presenting the structures in this book logically may at times suggest otherwise. The teacher's task is to make the 'present moment' of the drama significant, and to work in a sense to suspend plot. Ideally, as Suzanne Langer has recognized, drama does not deal with finished realities or events, but with future commitments and consequences. It will be the pressure of the future, in terms of the outcomes of past actions and decisions, which will give the drama its depth and purpose. The meanings embodied in a piece of drama will always be concerned with the notion of commitments and consequences, and the learning or changes in understanding associated with the experience will be likely to include this dimension.

Instead of a conventional narrative shape, these structures seek to present a cycle of experience. The development of the work does not necessarily proceed chronologically. Each phase of the structure may be oriented towards the past, present or future, as the teacher attempts to determine the needs and interests of the class, and the demands of the material on which they are working. The different phases in a particular structure need not be differentiated in an abrupt or arbitrary way.

An intense moment of debate or confrontation may be followed by a reflective phase oriented towards the past, or a planning phase where future possibilities are investigated. The teacher may sense in the class a need to explore the excitements of the present, or to reach back into the past in order to acquire more information and to build a stronger feeling quality, or to press forward in anticipation of future events.

Any of the different modes of dramatic activity may be used, to increase tension, provide a change of pace, or to strengthen or reflect on the experience, but a sense of time as it operates in drama will be crucial to these developing structures.

The drama may start firmly in the present, e.g. the reception of the emigrants on board the ship which will take them to the New World (Structure 11), or already possess an orientation towards the future, e.g. planning for the journey west, preparing for the arrival of the Indians (Structure 1). Next might come a change in direction towards the past, e.g. telling tales of previous exploits (Structure 12), re-creating a happy time now gone for ever (Structure 2), re-living one's arrest after a crime (Structure 4). Now, the drama may live intensely in the present, e.g. taking off in the starship (Structure 13), escaping from the work-house (Structure 4), choosing the person who will enter the haunted house (Structure 7). The orientations of these different phases of the work both back-wards and fowards in time will give significance to the drama and will help to organize the headlong rush of the action into an experience which has coherence and meaning.

Part 2   *The Structures*

Introduction

The practical examples in this book appear under two broad headings: Part 2: The Structures, and Part 4: Structures for Development. Each structure describes the course of an introductory lesson on a particular topic with an actual class and records the teacher's aims, the strategies employed and the pupils' responses. They represent some of the more successful efforts of a small number of teachers at a particular stage in their practice. Each structure has been attempted with more than one class, and the work inevitably took a different direction with each different group. In this section we outline how the material might be developed over a number of lessons using a variety of approaches.

A lesson commentary is given on the right-hand page, while the opposite page contains additional information and comment designed to help teachers deal with some of the problems that may arise in the course of setting up the work. In a wider sense, we hope that the points made will be of practical value in other situations and add to a personal vocabulary of teaching skills.

Where the work is based on an historical theme we give some background information and a list of books for further reading. It will not always be necessary for teachers to be particularly knowledgeable about the material at the outset of the lesson, though additional research may subsequently become desirable in order to identify the issues more clearly and open up a wider range of dramatic possibilities. The teacher's objective will be to lead pupils to a deeper understanding of the motives and feelings of the people involved and of the consequences of their actions, not simply to set up the precise re-enactment of a series of historical events.

Although we indicate the particular circumstances in which each of the lessons took place, for example, age of pupils, length of lesson and type of working area, these details should not be regarded as essential to the success of the work. It would be unwise to assume that the work will follow the same course in different hands and in different circumstances. We hope that the teachers will use these examples as a basis for work with their own classes rather than as any kind of rigid formula to be followed in exact detail. Teachers will obviously have to tailor the material, tasks and strategies to meet the needs and capabilities of different groups and their own teaching style and expertise. Many of the strategies outlined here are repeated in a variety of ways in the structures, and can be adapted to a variety of situations, subject matter and age groups.

Both 'Structures' and 'Structures for Development' suggest *possible* directions in which the work might develop, but it is likely that the drama will gain its own momentum once the children become absorbed by the topic. Teachers should be aware of and ready to follow up any fruitful ideas which arise even if the development of these ideas means moving away from the suggested plan.

Throughout, teachers will play a crucial part in guiding the work, pacing its growth and building on the pupils' contributions.

The pronouns *he/she* correspond to the sex of the teacher who led the specific lesson.

1 *The Way West*

INTRODUCTION

This topic, dealing with the movement of settlers across America in the middle of the nineteenth century, offers considerable scope for exploration through drama. In using this context, it will be possible to examine situations in which people take difficult decisions, tackle dangers and travel into the unknown in search of a better life. Through the framework provided, the pupils will be encouraged to put themselves in the position of these settlers, and to recreate some of the challenges which they had to face during their journey.

The pupils may approach this topic at first in an excessively action-oriented manner, and their view of the subject matter may be highly influenced by stereotypes from TV and films. It will be the teacher's task to engage the class in an exploration which goes deeper than these preconceptions, and which increases their understanding of the thoughts and feelings of people in such situations.

The greatest growth is likely to occur in the sections where the whole class are working together, while the small-group and pair work should help to deepen the drama.

There will be considerable opportunity for further research or reading on the topic by the pupils, and it should be possible to extend the experience through work in art, creative writing, history and individual research.

CONTEXT AND SOURCES

The movement of settlers seeking land to farm in the far west, travelling mainly by wagon train, began in the 1840s. The United States and Britain were hotly disputing the ownership of the North-west territories. If a sufficient number of Americans crossed to Oregon that territory would become American by right of occupation. Congress, the American governing body, had offered free land to every man who settled in Oregon and land for his wife and for each child. As farming land everywhere else had to be grabbed or bought, this was a wonderful offer. Frontier people who had already travelled to the Mid-West were now prepared to make the 2000-mile journey from the Mississippi–Missouri frontier to the Pacific Ocean.

The first group crossed to Oregon in 1841, but it was the great emigration of 1843 which established the pattern for later settlers and which solved the question of the ownership of Oregon by filling the area with Americans. In May 1843, 200 families and other emigrants, more than 1000 people in all, assembled near the town of Independence, knowing that Oregon had to be reached before winter.

Those with families travelled in canvas-covered wagons, many of which were ordinary farm wagons, about ten feet long by four feet wide. Buckets were hung under these carts, also water-kegs, lanterns, tools, and churns, while inside were clothes, pots, pans, rifles and bedding. The wagons were mostly dragged by oxen because these were stronger and more reliable than horses or mules. The settlers headed through the last outposts of civilization, the men driving the cattle while the women and children walked beside the wagons. Twenty miles was a good day's journey. The timing of the settlers' departure was crucial. The spring grass on the prairies had to be high enough to provide feed for the cattle and oxen, but if the departure was delayed too long they faced the danger of being trapped by snow in the mountains.

River crossings presented problems. The Platte River, for instance, was 'a mile wide and an inch deep', or so Mark Twain claimed. Another traveller said that it was 'too thick to drink and too thin to plough'. The bottom of the river was like a shifting quicksand in places, so it could be extremely treacherous, and often the heavy wagons got hopelessly stuck in the sand. The wagon train of 1843 took six days to cross the river, making rafts out of their wagon box tops by sewing buffalo hides together and stretching them across the tops. The sun dried the hides and the wagons carried the wives, children and goods safely across.

There were many other difficulties and dangers to be faced during the four- or five-month journey. Sickness and accidents were common. Medical aid was likely to be crude and the limited and monotonous diet led to much illness, including dysentery. Francis Parkman found a wooden plank by the side of the Oregon Trail which had the inscription:

> Mary Ellis
> Died May 7th, 1845
> Age two months

The old and the young were particularly vulnerable to disease. Wagons often broke down and axles cracked, and there was very little timber available to carry out repairs. The Indians also caused the settlers many problems, stealing livestock and harassing the wagon trains.

When the settlers reached the Willamette Valley in Oregon, they had much to do before winter closed in, in spite of their exhaustion after their long trek. The forests provided them with wood for houses and fences, and they were delighted to discover that they could plant crops immediately which would grow during the winter in the mild damp climate of Oregon. Their courage and endurance had brought them through the dangers and hardships of the journey to a new life in Oregon.

Further reading
Chandler, G. M., *The Way West*, The American Museum, Claverton Manor, Bath
Dickinson, Alice, *Taken by the Indians: True Tales of Captivity*, Franklin Watts, 1966
May, Robin, *The Wild West*, Macdonald Educational, 1975
Parkman, Francis, *The Oregon Trail*, Penguin, 1949
Schaeffer, Jack, *Shane*, Heinemann Educational Books, 1957
Stewart, George, *The California Trail*, Eyre and Spottiswoode, 1964
Twain, Mark, *Life on the Mississippi*, New English Library, Cygnet Classics, 1962
Van der Loeff, Rutgers, *Children on the Oregon Trail*, Puffin, 1963
Wilder, Laura Ingalls, *The Little House on the Prairie*, Puffin, 1964

TEACHING NOTES

I   This introductory discussion can be kept short. The facts provided by the teacher are a basis for the work. Any further factual information they may need can be introduced during the course of the work, or can be researched by the class between sessions.

2   This brief exercise should serve to start the class thinking about the theme. As their information is limited at this stage, the exercise may not produce much useful material. However, even in the short time which is allowed for this exercise, a number of interesting ideas can emerge. These will probably have to do with the reasons people might have for wanting to leave their homes, for instance those who have acquired a bad reputation and wish to make a fresh start, or those moving because of debts, evictions, bad luck in farming, or the death of close relatives.

The teacher need comment only briefly on this exercise, as there is likely to be an opportunity to develop these ideas later.

3   The fact that this is a male role need present no difficulty for female teachers. This is a fairly easy role to adopt, since it involves little more than being chairman of the meeting, and representing a person with some information and authority. It is important that the teacher should encourage the class to respond to the role as soon as possible, perhaps by asking them questions like 'Which of you people are already thinking about going to Oregon?' Then it will be part of the teacher's function in role to feed in information in response to questions from the class.

The status of the pupils in the activity can be raised and the value of their

INTRODUCTORY LESSON

This topic was explored with a first-year class in a drama
room for a sequence of double periods.

Objective
The teacher's objective was to embark upon a piece of drama which would occupy
the class for several weeks, providing scope for work of some depth, while also
providing contexts for dramatic action.

1   THE PEOPLE INVOLVED

Whole group
The teacher begins by showing the class the photograph at the beginning of this
topic. She asks them what the photograph suggests to them. In discussion, the
class decides that the photo shows travellers to the western states of America
about a hundred years ago. The people appear poor, and might be farmers.
Possible relationships between the people in the photograph are discussed. The
teacher gives the class a few historical facts about the pioneers who made the
journey to Oregon in the 1840s. A brief discussion about the reasons these people
might have for undertaking this dangerous journey is held.

2   REASONS FOR LEAVING

In pairs or threes
The teacher asks one person 'A' to choose to be one of the people shown in the
photograph, or someone of a similar type. Their partner 'B' is a friend, a colleague
or a relation of that person. A has heard about the wagon trains which are setting
off for Oregon and thinks it would be a good idea to go with them. B finds out the
reasons for A's decision.

   After a few minutes, the teacher asks each B to tell the rest of the class what they
have found out.

3   THE MEETING

Whole group
The class are sitting in a circle. The teacher asks them to imagine that they are in a
meeting place in a small town in the Mid-West. Perhaps it is the schoolroom, or a
church hall. She explains that she will be taking part in the next activity.

   She introduces herself as a representative of the government. She has come to
tell them about the opportunities which await them if they are prepared to make
the long journey to Oregon. The government will give them free farming land and
the country is extremely fertile. They will be much more prosperous if they
decide to move.

contributions recognized by suggesting that some of them may already possess considerable information and experience.

A rough sketch map of the proposed trail may be a useful visual aid for the teacher and will help to provide information and provoke questions about distance, terrain and possible dangers.

The class may be eager to make the decision immediately, without thinking very deeply about the journey which lies ahead. When the teacher brings this section of the work to an end she may need to point out that not enough is known about the people whom the class are pretending to be. If the class has a tendency to work rapidly and superficially, it is important that the teacher should help them to operate more thoughtfully and to build up roles and attitudes gradually.

Useful written tasks:

> A report in the local newspaper about this meeting.
> A poster advertising the government's offer of free land.

4   Some groups will develop the ideas contained in exercise 2. Several of the groups may already be working as families. In some of the other scenes members of the group can take on the non-migrant roles of landlords, friends or townspeople which they can discard when the journey starts. This changing of roles need not present a problem, though some groups may find it difficult.

5   From this point onwards it is important to stress that the work is about the people who *did* decide to make the journey. Otherwise, if the class remains divided on the issue, it may be difficult to proceed.

Again, the teacher's function here is that of chairman.

6   This list of belongings recurs later. If the group invents huge supplies of food and

She encourages the class to ask questions about Oregon, and the kind of journey they will have to undertake to get there. Questions focus on such subjects as the length of the journey, the dangers the travellers might face and the kind of life which would await them in Oregon. The teacher asks if any of those present have already travelled in the West and some of the class claim knowledge of the dangers and difficulties of the journey. The teacher's attitude is positive and she minimizes the dangers they are likely to face. She also stresses that those who decide to go must be hardworking and responsible people, because only people of this kind will survive.

The teacher does not rush the class towards a decision at this point, but asks them to think very carefully before making up their minds. They must consider what the journey will mean to them and what they will be leaving behind. They will meet again to make their final decision.

4   THE DECISION

Small groups
The teacher asks the class to get into groups of four or five. In one short scene can each group show the moment or the incident which caused them to make up their minds to risk the journey to the West? She stresses that these scenes will be important in providing information about the background of the people who made the journey and the kind of people they were.

After the scenes have been shown, the teacher comments briefly on them, drawing attention to the wide variety of motives people had for undertaking the journey, and the many different personalities who had to travel together for such a long time.

5   PLANS

Whole group
The teacher introduces this section of the work by saying that all the people who have decided to go on the journey must now meet together to make their final plans. As the government representative, she will accompany them to Oregon. They discuss the following questions:

> How should the journey be organized?
> Who will lead the settlers?
> What protection will they need on the journey?
> What should they take with them in their wagons?

6   THE WAGONS

Small groups
There is considerable excitement among the class, who are eager to begin the

weapons, this may weaken credibility and obstruct the development of the work. The teacher should stress that only the things which are listed actually exist. It may be more effective to discuss, as a class and not necessarily in role, the kind of essentials which would be needed for the journey.

It may be helpful to draw a ground plan of a wagon, showing the arrangement of the supplies and equipment.

As each wagon is visited, the teacher's purpose is to support and reinforce the pupils' belief and to challenge their thinking, as well as encouraging the development of their roles.

It is wise to encourage the pupils to adopt roles as adults or older adolescents. It will not be particularly helpful if they decide to be babies or very small children. Each group may have some imaginary members, for whom they are responsible, and these could be the very young members of the family.

7   This tableau, or still photograph, links with the very first activity of the lesson. The class begins to identify actively with the kind of people who were in the photograph that they first looked at.

8a   Before continuing with the work, the teacher will need to gauge the interest level of the class. If they seem eager to continue, this 'photograph' is a useful way of reminding them of the theme, and recalling the work to them. By subtly changing the 'photograph', it also allows the class to get the feeling that the journey has begun.

Ask the class to look at each group in turn, and encourage them to comment positively on each other's work. Their ability to observe and interpret body language, the arrangement of space, gesture and expression, should grow as the work proceeds.

journey as soon as possible. In order to make their work more thoughtful, the teacher stops the discussion and comes out of role. She indicates the actual size of a wagon, and ask the class to make lists of the essentials which they will take with them on the journey. Only the things which they have on their list will be taken with them, and these must all fit in their wagon.

In their groups, which now represent families, the class make a list of everything which will be required for the journey. Then each group selects a space in the room which will represent their wagon on the journey. They decide how their belongings are to be arranged, and how much space they will occupy. The teacher visits each group in turn and inspects their arrangements. During this phase of the work, roles are beginning to grow. Finally, the groups are fully prepared for their journey.

7 THE PHOTOGRAPH

Small groups
The teacher asks all the groups to arrange themselves by their wagon as if they were posing for a photograph. This is the moment when their journey is about to begin. From their expressions and the attitudes they adopt, is it possible to tell how high their hopes are, and to see their confidence and courage?

[The first double lesson ended here. This class were interested in pursuing the theme, and continued to work on it for several weeks.

Since this theme has a kind of narrative shape provided by the 'journey', it is important not to allow this linear development of story-line to take over. If it happens, the work may become merely a series of incidents – 'what happened next'. Instead, drama is likely to arise from moments of tension and decision, or when the settlers must face the consequence of their actions. If these moments of drama occur, the drama is likely to diverge considerably from the suggested structure, and the teacher must be prepared to take the work in a different direction.]

8 SETTING OUT

a *Small groups*
The next session might begin with the travellers re-creating the photograph with which the previous lesson finished. When each group has taken up its position, the teacher asks them gradually to alter their 'photograph' so that it shows what the settlers might look like after they had been on the trail for a month.

> Have they changed physically?
> Is it possible to tell whether their attitude to the journey has changed?
> How do they feel about each other now?

b   The switch to an individual statement should help pupils to build up their own roles, and reinforce their belief. If the class is not ready for individual commitment at this point, this is a strategy which can be used later in the drama.

9   This is the first opportunity for the groups to show some 'action'. The questions and comments after the scene, from the teacher and the rest of the class should help the groups to work thoughtfully.

10   At this point, groups may need time to engage in 'dramatic playing', to help them to develop belief in the life they are leading. The activities of the camp at evening may be usefully allowed to grow, and the teacher may remain part of the activity by finding reasons for visiting each group in turn. This kind of informal interaction will help them to sustain their roles and maintain the make-believe.

In this discussion, important questions may arise, and the teacher should listen carefully for anything which may provide a new development for the drama, and try to reinforce it. Some issues which are raised may be of a purely practical nature, requiring co-operation or problem-solving, but others may involve quite complex issues which will have considerable potential for the growth of the work. Such an issue might be a decision as to whether a sick family should be left behind, or whether the entire wagon train should risk delay for the sake of one wagon.

b *Individual work*
As each group holds its position for this second 'photograph', the teacher asks one
or two of the people in each group to speak their thoughts out loud.

What are they looking forward to in their new life?
What do they most fear in the months which lie ahead?
What do they miss from the life they have left behind?
Do they regret having begun the journey?

Alternatively, working in pairs, the pupils can share their thoughts and feelings
with one other person.

9 PROBLEMS

Small groups
In their previously-established groups, the teacher asks each wagon-party to
prepare and show an incident which happened to them during the first month of
their journey. This might be a problem to do with difficult terrain, bad weather,
poor health, loss of equipment or supplies, or anything else which occurs to the
groups. From this scene, which they will prepare and show to the rest of the class,
it should be possible to identify the problem clearly.

In discussion afterwards, the class may want to consider the following
questions:

Was the problem which arose anyone's fault?
How did the rest of the group react to the difficulty?
Did the group find a solution to their problem?
Can the rest of the wagon train learn from other groups' problems?

10 AROUND THE CAMP-FIRE

Whole group
This section can be introduced by the teacher providing a linking narrative:
'Every evening, the travellers arranged their wagons in a circle. They tended their
animals, carried out various chores and ate their simple supper. At last, they met
to talk over the events of the day, to try to solve any problems which had arisen
and to make plans for the next day's journey.'

The teacher, as one of the travellers, may conduct and co-ordinate the discussion which follows. As many people as possible should be encouraged to
contribute, even though this may take some time. If one of the pupils has been
chosen as leader of the wagon train, it may be possible for that pupil to chair the
meeting in role as leader, with the teacher's support and assistance.

The discussion will need to focus on any problems which have arisen during the
journey, perhaps to do with what has been shown in the previous scenes.

If the class seem eager to experience the excitement of an Indian attack, it may be wise to move on to later sections of this structure, where there are suggestions about handling this kind of encounter.

If the teacher has difficulty in deciding how to handle any ideas which have arisen, it may be wise to set the class a related task so that there is time to consider possible strategies.

Useful tasks might be:

A picture of the home they have left behind.

A map of the journey so far, including the various features they have encountered and the incidents which have occurred.

A diary of the journey.

11   This exercise offers another opportunity for thoughtful personal commitment. It may help some pupils if they are given time to draw the object which has such significance for them.

12*a*   The success of this section of the work may depend on the existing movement skills of the group. Some classes might find this task extremely difficult, in which case it would not be wise to attempt it.

b   The teacher should again be prepared for the drama to take a fresh direction during work of this kind. It is possible that serious accidents may occur, or that wagons or supplies may be lost. Unexpected events and their consequences must be accepted and included in the drama.

Problems of leadership may arise, or details of shared responsibility to do with the safety of the wagons, hunting, or looking after the animals. If no crucial problems arise, the camp-fire might be enlivened by singing or telling tales of adventures in the west.

It may be useful to establish the convention that the class sits in a circle for this meeting, and that people speak in turn, or that there is one spokesman for each wagon-group.

This is a part of the work in which the drama is likely to take a direction of its own, and the teacher must be prepared to accept and build on any interesting contributions from the class. It will not be possible to follow every lead which is offered, so the teacher will need to think carefully about the most fruitful way for the work to develop, and the best means of focusing on important issues.

11 THE PRECIOUS OBJECT

Individual work

The teacher reminds the class of the possessions they have brought with them in their wagons. In addition to that list of essentials, each person has brought one object with them from their previous life. It may be valuable, or it may be worthless, but is of great sentimental value. It is a link with the life they have left behind for ever. Each person in the class is asked to imagine that object as clearly as possible. Can they describe it to the rest of the class? Why is it of value to them? What does it remind them of?

The audience can be the whole group or they may work in pairs.

12 ON THE TRAIL

a *Small groups*

So far, each wagon will probably have been represented by a particular space in the room, or an arrangement of rostra or chairs. Is it possible for each group to convey a sense of the movement of the wagon, the animals and the people? The teacher might set this to the groups as a problem to be solved.

b *Small groups*

An alternative means of giving some sense of progression to the journey may be to ask each group in turn to take responsibility for leading the wagon train through a particularly difficult piece of the trail. The terrain could be marsh, rocks, quick-sands, mountains, rivers, narrow passes, etc. The leading group should plan their particular part of the journey, give all the necessary instructions to the other groups, and help to create the terrain they are passing through by their descriptions.

13   This kind of activity can be useful to start or finish a session, since it can remind the class of the concerns of the settlers, but does not necessarily move the drama forward. It allows for inventiveness and humour, as well as a change of approach to the theme.

14*a*   If the teacher feels that it may not be useful to change roles at this point, it is not strictly necessary. It will be possible for messages to arrive at the settlers' camp from the factor, giving the prices of supplies, and for these details to be passed on to the class by the teacher, if it seems better to remain in role as one of the settlers. If the teacher has decided *not* to work in role at all at this stage, the necessary information can be provided by a linking narrative.

b   It may become necessary for some families to sell the objects which they described earlier in the sequence, and which are of great personal value to them.

15   This activity will involve decision-making by the whole group, and planning in smaller groups. If the settlers decide that they cannot afford a feast for the Indians, they may be risking attacks later in the journey, or they may have to leave Fort Laramie before they have completed their preparations for the next stage of their journey.

13   DREAMS OF THE FUTURE

Small groups
The teacher may introduce this part of the work with a narrative link:
'Although the journey so far has been fraught with problems, the wagon train is approaching its first real resting-place, Fort Laramie. The settlers are beginning to feel hopeful once more and are still kept going by the dreams they have of the new life which awaits them in Oregon.'

   In small groups, the class is asked to prepare and show a dream sequence of the wonderful life which awaits them in Oregon. The scene may include both speech and movement, and should be exaggeratedly optimistic. It will provide opportunity for humour and exaggeration, as a contrast with the difficult lives which some of the settlers left behind.

14   FORT LARAMIE

a   *Whole group*
It may be helpful for the teacher to change role here and become the factor at Fort Laramie who will sell fresh supplies to the settlers, and give them new animals in exchange for their tired horses and oxen. The factor greets the wagon train and asks them to make camp outside the Fort.

   Supplies may be scarcer and more expensive than they anticipated. What does each group possess that can be traded for food, ammunition, fresh oxen and horses? Since the settlers are dependent on what is available at the fort, it is possible that the factor may exploit their weakness. What negotiations can they conduct with the factor?

   It may be that the factor demands further payment for the goods he provides.

b   *Small groups*
In groups, each family should decide which items are essential for the journey ahead. How can they pay for these items? Is there anything left in the wagons which they can use to trade with?

   It may be necessary to call a meeting of the whole wagon train, to discuss the problems which have arisen at Fort Laramie. Are any families in a particularly bad way? Can other groups help them?

15   THE FEAST

Whole group
The settlers discover that it is the usual practice for each wagon train which reaches Fort Laramie to entertain the local Indian tribes to a feast, in order to ensure their goodwill. That night it will be their turn. What can they spare from their stores to provide such a feast? The Indians may also expect presents. Each family must take part of the responsibility for this feast and decide what they can

It will probably not be wise to ask some of the class to become Indians at this stage of the work. Only one Indian, a representative of the whole tribe, is really necessary to receive the food and gifts of the travellers, and to respond to them. The Indian might be a member of the class, who has the ability to sustain such a role, an older pupil, a student or colleague, or the teacher changing roles again. The presence of an Indian may make this part of the work more significant, but is not absolutely necessary.

16   If necessary, the teacher might choose the moments to be illustrated, after discussion with the class, and set each group the same task. It will probably be interesting to compare the different groups' interpretations of the sequence of 'moments'. This kind of activity should increase their ability to select and shape scenes for presentation. The teacher will play a stage-managing function here, organizing the work of different groups, so that each sequence is presented with the minimum of fuss and confusion.

A diary entry including some details of what had been seen would be useful as a written follow-up to this task.

17   This kind of work may be useful with a group who are working too rapidly, and are concerned only with what happens next. To recall the past may succeed in slowing up their work and making it more thoughtful.

If the groups manage to include each other in their celebrations, it will make a change from showing their work, but may be more difficult to organize. In reflecting on this part of the work it may be worthwhile considering the changes which have occurred since that happy occasion. Have they any regrets about setting off for Oregon? Is there anything they can celebrate in a similar way on the journey? For example, if a Christmas celebration is chosen, each group might exchange presents in their own family, and then meet the other groups for a communal meal or a service.

18   This change of perspective on the work is likely to work best if it takes place at the beginning of a session.

It will probably assist the class in their change of roles if there is an introductory discussion about Indians and their life-style, attitudes and traditions. It may be helpful if the teacher can produce photographs and descriptions which will encourage the class to go beyond cliché and stereotype.

If the class are very committed to their roles as settlers it may prove difficult for them to alter their roles. If this is the case it may not be appropriate to work through this section.

spare, remembering that what might seem commonplace to them could seem precious or unusual to the Indians.

Each group brings its food and gifts to the meeting-place, in time for the feast. In turn, they each describe what they have brought, and present it formally to a representative of the Indian tribe. Alternatively, the food and gifts may be left for the tribe to collect at a later stage, once they have been described.

16   A DAY'S JOURNEY

Small groups
The travellers set off once more on their journey. To re-establish the sense of travelling, ask each group to select four or five different moments from a day's journey, and to present them as if they were 'stills' from a film, or illustrations in a book about wagon trains. These moments might include waking in the morning, a meal, hunting, herding the animals, moving through the heat of the day, an incident on the trail, and so on. The class will need to decide how each moment blends with the next, the best order for the 'moments', and so on. There should be no moving or speaking once the sequence has begun.

17   LOOKING BACK

Group work
The teacher provides a narrative link:
'The most difficult and dangerous part of the journey still lies ahead. The settlers and their animals are tired, and the going is slow. Spirits are no longer as high as they were, and the travellers are beginning to remember their past life with nostalgia and even regret.'

The teacher asks the groups to re-create one really happy occasion from their past life. This might be a wedding, a party, Christmas Day, or any other time which remains in their minds as being particularly happy. It may be possible for groups to interact while recalling their happy occasion, so that the improvisation develops an impetus of its own.

18   INDIANS

It is important for the teacher to gauge the interest of the class in the work at every stage. If they seem eager to continue with the theme, it may be valuable for them to alter the perspective by changing roles. If the teacher judges that they will be able to cope with this change of role, it should enrich their understanding of the theme, and challenge their ability to work within it. As settlers, they may have been aware of the presence of the Indians in the countryside through which they have been travelling. Now they must put themselves in the position of the Indians through whose territory they have been moving, and begin to try to imagine how the Indians thought and felt.

The work on Indians can be introduced in a number of ways. A member of the tribe may have seen the wagon train approaching and have reported this news to the council. As described opposite, a member of a neighbouring tribe may bring news of the settlers, or a written message may have been received by the tribe.

The language and bearing of the Indians will be very different from that of the settlers. The teacher will be aiming to encourage a sense of dignity in the group and will model this in language and gesture as part of the role that has been undertaken.

A useful exercise which may help the pupils to believe in their new roles may be to ask them to decide on an Indian name for themselves – a name which will reflect their skills, qualities or position in the tribe.

The teacher may be working to delay action in this section, since it is possible that the class may be eager for the satisfaction of engaging in a violent attack on the wagon train.

19   This part of the work is designed to give the pupils the satisfaction of action-oriented drama, which they may have been anticipating from the theme. At the same time, the 'battle' must be highly controlled. Since they are showing what happened on a previous occasion, they can have the enjoyment of 'dying' dramatically, and of engaging in violent action without the development of the rest of the work being affected.

Whole group

The teacher asks the class to arrange themselves as they think Indians would await a meeting with a member of another tribe. A messenger arrives from a neighbouring tribe and asks to speak to the Indians. This tribe has been watching the journey of the settlers and has come to enquire what their neighbours mean to do about the wagon train. If the teacher wishes to work in role, she can take on this function.

The group, of whom ideally the teacher is one, discuss the presence of the wagon train, and its significance for the tribe. The teacher can help to focus the discussion on such questions as:

What has been noticed about the wagon train?
How do the white settlers behave?
In what ways are they different from Indians?
Has anyone ever met a white person?
Does anyone remember a previous occasion on which a wagon train crossed
    the territory?
What happened to it?
What action should be taken about this wagon train?
Has its presence affected the Indian way of life?

This section may take some time to work through. As many as possible of the group should be encouraged to express their opinions. In questioning the group, the teacher may be able to encourage them to include imaginary events from the past in what they say, for example, previous encounters with white traders or trappers or explorers, or legends they have heard about the white people.

This decision-making session should be allowed to continue while the opinions and arguments are still being offered. The meeting can be brought to an end before a decision is actually reached. One way of postponing the decision may be to say:
'The council has a difficult decision to make. Let us wait until sunset to make our decision. Each member of the tribe will return to his tent. We must think very carefully what we should do, and ask the Great Spirit to give us guidance. We will meet again in council at sunset.'

19 MEMORIES OF BATTLE

If, in the previous section, it has become obvious that other previous wagon trains have been attacked, a narrative link by the teacher will reinforce this idea and help to introduce the next part of the work:
'As the tribe sat alone in their tepees, some of them remembered what had happened when a wagon train had crossed their land the season before. The tribe had held a great council and the warriors of the tribe decided that they must attack the strangers and drive them from their lands. Their courage was great and they fought with all their skill, but many of the finest warriors of the tribe did not return from that battle.'

a   The more carefully the 'battles' are prepared, the more effective they will look. Encourage the class to work towards an almost choreographed effect, perhaps by moving in slow motion, or exaggerating the effect of every gesture.

b   This kind of exercise allows reflection on the 'battle', and should help pupils to consider the effect of war on a people.

Instead of a survivor of the battle, one person might have been an onlooker at the event.

20   The teacher might be able to indicate the kind of guidance which the tribe received from the Great Spirit by recounting an example of a dream which gave the tribe some important warning on a previous occasion.

If the class are asked in turn what they dreamed of, they may be able to interpret their dreams as warning signs.

It may be wise to have an actual letter from the stranger already prepared. This could be written in English, or in some kind of pictogram.

If the tribe decide not to receive the stranger, or to treat him with hostility, this may provide for further developments within the work. The choice of someone to take on the role of stranger will depend on this decision. It will be clearly less demanding to be the recipient of gifts and a spectator at a ceremonial than someone who must respond to the antagonism of the tribe.

a   *Group work*
The teacher divides the class into large groups and asks them to prepare and show
what happened when the Indians attacked the previous wagon train. They will be
re-creating an event that has become part of the tribe's history, so their courage
and ferocity in battle will be obvious and may even be heroically exaggerated.
Some of the group will need to be the members of the previous wagon train who
are attacked by the Indians.

These scenes should be shared with the rest of the class. In reflection on these
battles, the teacher may need to emphasize the qualities which will feed belief in
the work and the new roles they have adopted. For example, skill in fighting,
co-operation, stealth, courage, etc.

b   *In pairs*
A survivor of that last battle talks to a younger member of the tribe who was not at
that battle and describes what it was like and the effect the battle had on the tribe
as a whole. Did the council take the right decision? Was fighting the only
alternative? Can they risk another battle?

20   THE COUNCIL AT SUNSET

Whole group
The tribe meet in council once again, to make a decision about the most recent
wagon train. With the memory of the previous battle now fresh in their minds,
what decision will they come to? Can they afford to lose any more of their best
warriors? Might it be possible to negotiate with the settlers?

The teacher, as one of the tribe, perhaps an elder, may ask the group if any of
them have received guidance from the spirits while they rested in their tepees.
Their tribe has always been guided by the images which the Great Spirit sent to
them in their dreams. Have any of the tribe now received signs or warnings?

At an appropriate point in the discussion, the teacher may choose to introduce
the fact that a letter has been received from a white man, asking if he can visit their
camp. Each teacher may decide individually on the way in which the letter has
reached the tribe. It may have been left at the edge of the camp, to be found by the
tribe, or it may have been given to one of the children of the tribe by a white
stranger.

The tribe must decide if they will receive the stranger. If he is to be welcomed,
what form should this welcome take? It may be important not to antagonize the
visitor, but at the same time to show him the strength of the tribe and its customs
and culture. If the council decide to welcome him with a great display, then this
will have to be prepared for very carefully.

If the teacher can encourage the class to come to the decision of welcoming the
stranger, it should have the effect of providing them with the opportunity of
building up the life and culture of the tribe. If they agree, the work can proceed as
follows:

21   The teacher will have an important stage-management function here. The welcoming of the stranger and the ceremonial with which he is greeted should proceed smoothly, once it has begun, with everyone maintaining their roles and attitudes.

The teacher will need to decide in what order the groups present their work, and how each activity is begun and ended. It may be useful for the tribe to be seated together in a semi-circle, and for each group in turn to rise and present their work.

22   Again, the discussion in role on these questions will need to echo the formality and ceremonial of the previous section.

It might be interesting to consider how the treaty could be written or drawn so that both Indians and settlers could understand it.

23   It should probably be left to individual pupils to decide if they wish to remain as Indians or resume their roles as settlers.

Those who choose to be settlers again will probably find it more useful if they become the younger adults among the settlers. They don't necessarily have to work in the same groups as they did when they were settlers earlier. Those who wish to remain as Indians might choose to enact the Indians' version of how the settlers got left behind – perhaps emphasizing their carelessness or lack of know-ledge of conditions on the trail. Working without words should help to simplify the scene and highlight the movement qualities of what is happening.

21   WELCOMING THE STRANGER

Small groups
The teacher divides the class into small groups, and asks each group to be responsible for one of a variety of activities, which will be presented as part of the tribe's welcome to the white stranger. These activities might include:

A display of hunting skills	The exchange of gifts
A war dance	A great feast
A mock battle	Music and drumming
A sacrificial ritual	A dance to the Great Spirit

When the different activities are fully prepared, the stranger is welcomed to the tribe's meeting-place. The role of white stranger may be taken by one of the class, a colleague, student or older pupil. The welcome should be highly ceremonious, and possess a sense of formality.

22   THE TREATY

Whole group
As a result of the feast, it may be that peace is established for the moment between the settlers and the Indians. The tribe meets in council with the white stranger to decide what arrangements can be made between them, so that they can co-exist peacefully while the wagon train is crossing the Indian territories.

Will it be possible for the Indians and the settlers to draw up a formal treaty between them? What conditions should it include? How will it be enforced?

23   LOST ON THE TRAIL

Small groups
It should be possible for Indians and settlers to meet each other at this point in the work, without the danger of stereotyped reactions to the situation. Ask the class to recall the difficulties which the settlers experienced on their journey. Although in recent sessions they have been thinking as Indians, some of them will now have the opportunity to resume their roles as settlers. Using a narrative link, the next task may be introduced as follows:
'The wagon train has been travelling forward on its journey. Now, it has reached one of the most difficult parts of the trail. At this point, a group of young people has become separated from the main party, and has been left behind. Perhaps they went hunting, a wagon broke down, they got lost while searching for straying cattle, or a storm overtook them.'

The teacher asks the class to get into small groups. Can they show, in a scene without words, how these young people became separated from the rest of the wagon train?

She asks the class to choose the explanation which seems the most likely version of what happened, and which they wish to accept as the truth.

24   When the meeting between both groups has occurred, perhaps engineered by the teacher, or initiated by the pupils, it should be possible to allow the pupils to take responsibility for handling the meeting and its outcome.

a and *b*   If there are an uneven number of settlers and Indians, this exercise can be carried out in groups of three or four. The basic task will remain the same – a training exercise. Through it, the pupils will be deciding what they value about the Indian way of life, or later, when the exercise is repeated, defining some of the skills and values of the white people.

With a group who are capable of working in depth, it might be interesting to set more complex tasks for them to share. For example, explaining their ideas about religion to each other, or telling each other something of the history of their respective peoples.

25*a*   Again, this rescue allows opportunities for action, but action which has a reflective element as part of it.

b   The reflection in role about the Indians and their way of life is continued in this task.

Now the class must decide which of them would like to be the young settlers who have been left behind, and which of them wish to remain as Indians.

24   COLLABORATION

Narrative link:
'Because of the difficult country in which they found themselves, it was impossible for the young settlers to continue their journey straight away. They would have to remain with the tribe for a time.'

Whole group
The Indians have seen the plight of the young settlers who have been left behind. How do they approach these strangers in their territory? Are they warlike and aggressive, or do they remember the treaty which has been signed? Both groups are likely to be somewhat suspicious of each other. The settlers may need the help of the Indians if they are to continue their journey and rejoin the wagon train. How can they persuade them to help?

a   *In pairs*
One is an Indian and one is a settler. The Indian begins to teach the white settler some of the skills of the tribe – hunting, tracking, skinning buffalo, making tepees, etc. The pupils who have chosen to be the settlers then display their skills to the rest of the group. How well have they learned Indian ways? Can they fit in with the tribe's way of life? How should they be treated? Are they guarded by the tribe or can they be trusted to come and go as they please?

If they are accepted into the tribe, who will be responsible for them? Is there any way in which they can be useful to the tribe? What can be learned from them?

b   *In pairs*
Now the partner who has been the settler teaches the Indian one of the skills of the settlers – how to use a rifle, how to sew or bake bread, how to build a wagon or a log cabin, how to read or write.

25   RESCUE

a   *Small groups*
The settlers are rescued from the Indians. In small groups, show how this might have happened. Did the rescuers understand the situation? Did they realize the position of the settlers within the tribe? Was it easy for the settlers to leave the tribe? What had their life there meant to them?

b   *In pairs*
One person has returned from the tribe, and is talking to a friend or relation, who

26   This celebratory occasion is a chance for the group to reflect more generally on all the work they have done on this theme, and is a means of giving significance to the discoveries they may have made about the theme and about themselves during the drama.

27   This last exercise is again an opportunity for reflection on all the work which has been done on this theme.

has very fixed and narrow views about the Indians. Can the friend be helped to a better understanding of what Indians are like, through hearing about these first-hand experiences?

26 THE NEW LAND

Narrative link
'All the settlers arrived safely in Oregon. They worked hard in the first year, clearing the land, building log cabins, planting crops. At Thanksgiving-time, a year after their arrival, they met together to celebrate and give thanks for their new life.'

In a large group, can each person say what the journey has meant to them?

27 REMEMBERING

In pairs or threes
The settlers who went to Oregon are now old people, and many years have passed since the journey. Can they tell their grandchildren about their experiences on the journey, so that they will understand what this undertaking meant to them?

2 *Leaving Home*

This structure suggests a variety of ways in which teachers can set up work on a topic which frequently proves to be a popular choice with pupils in the mid-secondary age-group. The material is organized in two parts.

Initial activities will help pupils to look at the reasons which make young people leave home. The investigation takes place in the context of an agency which helps youngsters who come to the city without funds, work or accommodation. As voluntary workers in the agency, the pupils can pursue the theme in a number of directions: looking into the past to identify the reasons for leaving, staying with the current predicament of the person involved and moving into the future to test out possible courses of action. The volunteers' 'training sessions' will allow pupils to adopt a variety of roles.

Subsequent developments focus on a group of homeless young people living in a hostel which provides short-stay accommodation. For most of this section pupils will be required to maintain and develop one role.

Many of the strategies once again rely upon teachers' willingness to operate from within the drama, first as one of the senior workers in the agency and then as Houseparent in the hostel. Both roles allow them to remain in a position where they can organize, encourage and support the pupils' contributions and develop the drama according to their interests.

SOURCE MATERIAL

At the age of 16, young people can legally leave home with parental consent. (In Scotland the age limit is 16 with or without parental consent.) Children under legal age who are subsequently reported as missing persons can be returned to their parents if found by the police.

Those who arrive in London can seek advice and support from agencies which cater for the young homeless. Some may be able to find temporary accommodation in a short-stay hostel, and so gain a kind of breathing space which allows them to sort out what they want to do next now that they have gained some independence. While in the hostel they may be able to look for work, arrange social security benefits and seek permanent accommodation: at best a flat shared with others but sometimes a long-term hostel, a hotel or a squat. Hostel facilities are likely to be of a very basic nature with the residents sharing a multi-bedded room or having only a cubicle of their own.

It is a pity the media don't highlight the plight of the young people I meet a little more. Sadly, they are not considered interesting enough – they do not smash up trains or assault guards, mug old ladies or take drugs. They don't shoplift down Oxford Street or sell themselves at Piccadilly. They are mostly sensible young people who cannot find a reasonable place to live, a place to call home.

Tony Gower, 'Alone in London Service Annual Report, 1979–80'

Young people talking
Susan: My father died when I was four and my mother remarried when I was eleven. I didn't get on with my step-father at all. He was a violent sort of person. When he came in, it was always "you do what I say", kind of thing. I was very rebellious at that age. I was determined he wasn't going to tell me what to do. I went home one night and found my bags packed. I was 15 years old. It was a build-up of all the trouble over the previous months. I was never there much and never did what I was told. It was as much my fault as anyone else's.

Sean: I first ran away because I was having arguments with my dad over money and over staying in. Every time I wanted to go out, he'd interrogate me and he wouldn't give me money. I was fed up. I'd planned on running away before but I'd never plucked up the courage. I thought, 'Well, I'll do it this time', so I got my suitcase, got the train to Dublin, the boat to Holyhead and then I hitch-hiked to Chorley in Lancashire – that's my home town. I met this other lad on the train and he was running away as well.

Pam Schweitzer, *A Place of My Own*

I don't know what it is that makes me run off. It's when something gets me, if something gets through to me – not just anything but it can be a little thing. (Tracy on the run)

Cheryl ran away at sixteen. A month before, her mother had walked out of the family home, leaving her father who's a milkman, her younger brother and herself. 'My mum and dad were always rowing, they rowed all the time. I don't know what about, not about another man. I used to think my mum was right, I don't know. I hate her. They rowed about the housekeeping, when he put it down to keep her in at nights. I don't know where she went, she just went out. She'd go but she always said she'd take me with her. The night she went, a Friday, they had a flaming row and she packed up and she went. I was crying on the kitchen floor.

One night I went to a girlfriend's engagement party and I rang her. She said meet her in town at eleven o'clock. I had my case and I waited for her and she never came. I was terrified on my own in town at eleven o'clock at night. I went back to the party and stayed with my girlfriend. I couldn't go home, my dad's got a terrible temper when he's up. Next day I came down here. . . .' (Cheryl and family strife)

Angela Willans, *Breakaway*

On leaving home a young person is likely to be in a state of great emotion and excitement. Realisation of some of the difficulties and loneliness of life in London and other large cities may take some weeks, and it is during this period that he or she is most vulnerable to exploitation. Quite a number want to return home after two or three weeks, having made their gesture of independence.

DHSS, 'Working group on homeless young people', July 1976 – HMSO

Leaving home for London was often seen as a reaction against parental authority. They (the subjects interviewed) mentioned their desire for 'freedom' and 'independence'.

Many left home on an exploratory basis, knowing they could return (for instance, resume living with parents). Most felt that they were leaving a nothing-to-stay-for or at least a nothing-to-lose situation, although after arrival they soon began to appreciate and miss people and things previously taken for granted: friends, home comforts, a familiar environment. Quite a few knew or guessed that the agencies provided a safety net.

D. Brandon *et al.*, *The Survivors*

The evils of Piccadilly can still achieve front-page status. Articles on under-age prostitution raise nothing more than shocked murmurs, but the reality is that weekly in London hundreds of homeless young people move through the network of statutory and voluntary services in order to survive. The agencies are as varied as the clients they serve – both frequently under-achieve.

(A survey of just over one hundred young people selected during the years 1974–6 from among the users of three London projects offering emergency accommodation.)

The people who form our client group often come from a background of deprivation. The agencies where they seek help are similarly affected. Dwindling resources and increasing competition inhibit our effectiveness. Bed-finding is in danger of becoming a sacred cow, for that in itself is often a lengthy and arduous task. Worker and client together, we share the frustrations of finding somewhere to live and a job. A bed is found, a job follows. The principal objectives are achieved. But the struggle for many is not over.

Tony Gower, 'Alone in London Service Annual Report 1979–80'

'I thought when I came to London my life would change. I'd heard all sorts of stories . . . big fantastic place; all big flashing lights . . . plenty of everything, it's all a pack of lies. . . . It's just the same as anywhere else only it's a bigger place.'

'Everything is on top of me. I'm frightened by the size of London. I've made no friends at all. I wouldn't have come if I'd known what it was like. London. It's the place you make for when you're running away . . . it's big, you can get lost in it.'

'What shall I do next? I'm really scared, I mean I'm out in the big world, fifteen and on my own . . . I want to go home but I don't want to go home. I don't want to go because I know what it's like at home but I don't want my mum to worry . . . I'm going to start crying in a moment. . . . I need someone a lot older, older and wiser than me to sort my troubles out.'

D. Brandon et al., The Survivors

Those arriving in London with sufficient money had usually stayed in cheap bed and breakfast or very basic hotel accommodation until their money had run out. One male stayed one night in an expensive hotel which made him destitute on his second day . . . One female found a place in a squat on her first day and stayed for five weeks before it was pulled down. Two young girls, both running away from home, avoided the agencies rather than run the risk of being returned home.

One slept rough for two weeks. . . .

D. Brandon et al., The Survivors

Young people talking
Glen: They've been really good to me in this hostel. I've mixed in well and got on with everybody. I was only supposed to stay for 3 weeks but they let me stay for 7 weeks. It took that long for me to find a place but now I'm happy about where I'm going. I want to stay there for about a year. I'm trying to get work and I'll sign on with the council and try to get myself a flat.

Andy: I like it in this hostel. I'm comfortable here for a while. They're all really friendly – you get talking straight away. I signed on yesterday and I'm looking for a bedsit. I want to be independent and sort myself out.

Alison: I found living in a hostel was all right, but all the time you're there you've got the worry that you've got to move on soon and they're not going to take you for much longer. I mean you've got the headache of looking for somewhere else again. Another thing: some hostels are too much like establishments, if you know what I mean. You might go and tell the workers you've got a problem and you want help with it but you feel they've heard it a million times before. You're just another case to them, just a number more or less. That's how it feels anyway. It's awful really.

Tony: I stayed at a short-term hostel in the West End of London. It's just for 3 nights and it's for young people under 21. The idea is to go there and sort out your social security and hopefully get into a Bed and Breakfast from there or into a long-term hostel. They did at least help me to get my four weeks' money sorted out.

Some of the hostels I looked at were unbelievable. One had 18 people to a small room and they were charging £18.75 a week without food. Lots of them were overcrowded. You just couldn't live in them. I reckon a good hostel would be where there was no more than four to a room and where they really try to help you get personally involved, you know.

Pam Schweitzer, A Place of My Own

FURTHER READING

Brandon, D., Wells, K., Francis, C., and Ramsey, E., *The Survivors*, Routledge & Kegan Paul, 1980
Community Service Volunteers, *No Bed No Job*, CSV Teaching Pack, 1978
Deakin, Michael, and Willis, John, *Johnny Go Home*, Quartet Books, 1980
Fairbrother, Nan, *Shelter*, Connexions, Penguin Books, 1972
Rae, M., Hewit, P., and Hugill, B., *First Rights*, National Council for Civil Liberties, 1979
Schweitzer, Pam, *A Place of My Own*, ILEA Learning Materials Service, 1982
Toomey, Lee, *Down and Out*, New Citizen Books, Wayland, 1973
Willans, Angela, *Breakaway: Family Conflict and the Teenage Girl*, Temple Smith, 1977

ORGANIZATIONS

Alone in London Service, West Lodge, 190 Euston Road, NW1 2EF
Community Service Volunteers, 237 Pentonville Road, London N1
Shelter, 157 Waterloo Road, London SE1

TEACHING NOTES

The group had worked in this way on previous occasions but had sometimes found difficulty in listening to each other's contributions. The teacher is aware that this problem can be intensified with the class operating as one large group, but is prepared to use the strategy here in order to be in a position to press for the kind of seriousness he wants.

1a   The teacher chooses to give the pupils roles as *trainee* helpers for the following reasons:

> It allows them to remain at one remove from the material if they find it disturbing.
> It allows them the freedom of not really having to know how such helpers would operate. They are only volunteers and amateurs and therefore unskilled in the task they are about to undertake.
> It allows him to use the same pupils in a variety of situations and roles within the framework of the 'training session'.

The teacher's principal concerns at this point in the lesson are to get the pupils accustomed to working together and to use the drama activities to illustrate, in action, some of the reasons which make young people leave home.

INTRODUCTORY LESSON

This structure was tried with a group of second-year girls in a classroom for a series of single periods.

Objective

The teacher wanted to set up a framework which would provide support and motivation for a class whose members found it difficult to pursue work seriously without careful guidance. He had planned a number of clear and limited tasks which would not make too many demands on the girls. He would also give help and encouragement from within the drama by taking on a role himself.

Introduction

The teacher asks the class if they would be prepared to do some work on the kind of problems which make young people leave home. With their agreement he begins to talk about the reasons which might prompt teenagers to make such a decision. The pupils offer their contributions. The teacher then explains that he will start the drama in role with the class working as one group. They will need to listen carefully to what is being said and pick up the clues which will give them an idea of the situation.

1 THE TRAINING SESSION

a *Whole group*

The teacher asks the pupils to arrange their chairs in a circle. He introduces himself as one of the workers in an agency which provides help and advice to young people who have left home and are recently arrived in the city. He welcomes the pupils as a group of volunteers who are prepared to help in the agency. They will obviously need some kind of training before they can begin their work. As part of this first session he asks if five or six of them will agree to take on the roles of some teenagers who have come to the agency for help. Six pupils offer to take on this task and the teacher asks each one to decide on the main reason which has made them leave home. He reminds them of the ideas raised in the initial discussion, for example, arguments with parents and step-parents, disagreements with brothers and sisters, failure to get work or to do well at school, a desire for independence.

He asks the six 'teenagers' to move their chairs out of the circle and sit in another part of the room. He then gives the following instructions to the volunteers: 'Remember that although this is only a training session to help you in your work, I shall expect you to carry out your tasks as if you were really dealing with youngsters who have come to us for guidance. The first thing you must do is to interview these teenagers and find out as much as you can about their background, why they have left their families, whether they now think they have made the right decision and what they plan to do. Some of these people may be feeling a

b Each group is assigned to one of the six clients. No group is allowed to begin until the teacher has completed the organization of the task.

Though each group is aware of the teacher's presence he only intervenes in those instances where the volunteers seem to be having difficulties in asking the right questions or where there is embarrassment, laughter or behaviour that is likely to disturb groups working nearby. All his contributions are made in role. He gives a lot of encouragement.

c The girls who role-play the clients all adopt an age that makes them several years older than they actually are. This is a form of distancing that teachers might well employ deliberately if they feel that the material is likely to prove unsettling for some members of their class.

d Each situation involves only a few people at a time. The remaining members of the group are observers who are subsequently invited to comment on what they have seen, suggest alternative courses of action and introduce other characters into the story. The teacher can control the development of the work from his place in the circle. He can ask questions which may help pupils to think more deeply about the events portrayed or ask for a replay of the scene, perhaps focusing in on a specific action or comment.

little lonely or afraid. You may need to be tactful and show that you would like to help if possible. We'll meet together shortly to discuss what you've found out.'

b *Small groups*
The class divides into small groups. They take their chairs to sit with the clients, and the head of the agency wishes them luck in their interviews.

The volunteers talk to the teenagers. The teacher moves around the group helping to focus the questions and give support to those who are playing the runaways. He stresses the seriousness of the task in those groups where this seems to be lacking. (On the whole these interviews were conducted with quiet concern and both sides seemed to have few problems in keeping them going.) After ten minutes or so clients and volunteers are asked to return to the large circle.

c *Whole group*
The head of the agency thanks the six individuals for making their roles so believable and commends the volunteers on the way in which they have carried out their initial tasks. He asks them to report back on their discoveries and tell their colleagues of any difficulties they have encountered. The volunteers begin to provide detailed case-histories of the six clients. Where further information is needed, or where points need clarification, the head talks directly to the pupil taking on the role of the person under discussion. He invites other members of the group to do the same until the whole class has a clearer picture of the six teenagers concerned. The head of the agency is pleased with the volunteers' progress.

d *Small groups*
In role, the teacher asks the group which case they would like to look at in greater detail. He explains that since drama techniques are used as part of the helpers' training programme, this kind of demonstration will be quite easy to set up here at the agency.

The group want to examine, in this case, the story of a girl who had been living with her mother and step-father. After a series of disagreements she had gone to stay with her father but he was living with somebody else and the girl had not been made welcome. For this reason she had decided to seek an independent life.

The teacher asks the pupil role-playing the girl if she will agree to continue with her story. He tells the class that he will set up the situations that they would like to look at – those that will give them a more detailed picture of events.

They want to see the girl at home with the mother and step-father. Two pupils volunteer to take on these roles and the teacher asks the client to suggest the kind of situation which invariably led to an argument. The scene is played and the teacher then invites the observers' comments and suggestions. A number of situations are set up involving different people in the girl's story. For example, mother and daughter alone together, mother and step-father talking about the

2   The repetition of this format depends largely on the pupils' agreement to work in this way for another lesson. Some may find it difficult to do so. They may be seeking a greater variety of experience. However, where groups are keen to examine each case history in turn, the teacher would do well to capitalize on their interest.

As an alternative to working in one large group, the teacher can divide the class into smaller groups and ask them to carry out their own investigations using the example of the first lesson as a guide. Each group works with one of the individuals who has left home. They set up their own situations and conduct their own enquiry. At the end of the session the groups share their findings with the rest of the class.

It would be unwise to adopt this strategy with classes who cannot operate effectively when divided into small groups and left to their own devices.

3a   The pupils who have taken on the roles of the original clients may be prepared to stay with these roles. If they choose not to do so, the teacher will need to enlist the help of another group of pupils to represent a different set of clients.

It may be necessary to limit the amount of furniture used for this activity. Some children may become so preoccupied with the task of building 'the office' that they are unwilling to move on to the next phase of the drama. A table and some chairs should be sufficient for each group.

girl, father and daughter discussing whether or not she can stay with him. Though the central role is played by the same pupil, the others are represented by various members of the class. The scenes lead up to the final incident which prompts the girl to leave.

The first lesson ended with a brief discussion about this particular case history. Some pupils were keen to pin blame on the adults concerned, but others pointed out that there were faults on all sides.

The lesson format proved useful in providing the pupils with specific, achievable tasks each set within a framework which allowed the teacher to control the development of the work without interrupting the course of the drama.

The theme was subsequently developed in a number of ways.

2   HELPING OTHER CLIENTS

The head of the agency conducts a further training session. This time the volunteers examine the case histories of the other clients.

a The remaining clients each tell a part of their story.

b The group selects one person whose life they will now look at in greater detail.

c The pupils suggest the situations they would like to see, based on what they know of the person so far. The development of the scenes is not planned in advance. They are performed within the circle of observers.

d The observers give advice, make comments and suggest ways in which confrontations might have been avoided.

3   AN ATTEMPTED RECONCILIATION

a *Small groups*

The agency tries to bring about a reconciliation between the clients and their families. The teacher (in role as the head of the agency) explains that although this kind of situation rarely happens at the agency itself, it will be useful for the volunteer helpers to know how to deal with it should the occasion arise.

The class divides into small groups, one to each client. They choose pupils to represent members of the family. These may have been seen already in the previous role-play sessions, but they need not necessarily be played by the same pupils here. There will also be one or two agency helpers in each group and, of course, the client.

The helpers set up their offices. They have the responsibility for conducting the meeting in whatever way they feel to be appropriate, but may be asked to consider the following points:

Will the helpers talk to both parties individually before bringing them together?

How much information do the helpers need to know beforehand?

How will they go about finding out what they don't know?

b   The teacher can ask that all the interviews begin at the same time and so avoid the kind of disruption that occurs when some groups begin the drama whilst others are still at the planning stage.

c   If the clients are new to their roles little will be known about them in advance. This information has to be gained in the course of the interviews. It does not matter if there are conflicting stories from each of the parties concerned.

If groups are not coping well with this task it might be more profitable for the teacher to stop the activity, call them all together and set up a demonstration interview in which he can take on a role. His example may help pupils to acquire the appropriate attitudes and give them an indication of the kind of questions they will need to ask.

d   The aim is to provide a variety of situations which will help pupils to look at individual cases in greater detail. The teacher may need to adopt his usual role as the head of the agency so that he can have access to the interviews and direct them along a particular line of enquiry.

The drama work can be supplemented by material from a range of sources: factual information based on newspaper articles, statistical reports, poems, stories and plays, etc.

How tactful and considerate will the interviewers need to be?
What advice do they think they can give?

The helpers are not expected to achieve a reconciliation as the result of just one meeting. They will be concerned to get the individuals talking to each other, to identify their differences and perhaps get them to think of ways in which these could be resolved.

b *Whole group*
The interviews are brought to a close and the groups meet to compare notes. The discussion can be conducted with the pupils and the teacher operating either in or out of role. The helpers are encouraged to share the problems they have faced and the kind of advances they feel have been made. They may be able to comment on the possibilities of a reconciliation between the teenagers and their families.

c *Small groups*
The groups reconstruct part of their interview to show to the rest of the class. If time allows, the meeting could be shown in its entirety. Alternatively, particular moments could be selected for presentation. For example:

— the point in the meeting when reconciliation looked most likely.
— the point in the meeting when it really seemed as if there was no way of bringing these people together.

d *Small groups: further work*
If the pupils are keen to continue with the interviews a series of further meetings can be set up. For example:

i   The client and members of the family meet on another occasion. Have attitudes changed?
ii   An agency helper gives individual advice to a member of the family or to the client. In what ways do these more intimate interviews differ from the others?
iii   Friends are brought to the agency in an attempt to bring about a change of mind and get the client to return home.
iv   One of the clients is ready to return home. The agency makes further contact with the family. Are they still prepared to take back the runaway or have they, too, reversed their former opinions?

The preceding activities will have offered a range of experiences illustrating some of the reasons which make young people leave home without parental consent. The information gained during the course of these activities can be used to support pupils in the next phase of the work which now takes on a slightly different direction. For most of the time they will be asked to adopt and maintain one role.

4*a*   This strategy could form an alternative starting-point to the topic. The kind of
hostel that the teacher has in mind is the type that provides short-stay accommodation for a small number of residents. They may live there for a few months while
looking for work and trying to find a more permanent base.

The plan shows the layout of the hostel (a large house?). The bedrooms are already
clearly marked but the use to which the other rooms will be put is not designated in
advance. This allows the teacher to turn the common areas into the kind of spaces
the pupils are asking for. For example, 'Yes, there is a television room. It's the one
shown here just by the kitchen.' He completes the plan by writing up what each
room will be used for.

   The teacher should be careful not to adopt an ultra-authoritarian stance. Though
it is possible that the inmates may ultimately come to rebel against the hostel
regime it is not especially productive for them to do so at this early stage.

   b   Some pupils may remain in the roles adopted during the previous work.
Others may need time to think of the role they will represent.
   The teacher can set a limit on the time available for each pair discussion. At a
given signal the pair separates and the individuals move on to find another partner.

   c   The pupils should be asked to use their real first names. This can avoid
confusions within the drama.
   Though this activity make take time to complete, especially with a very large
class, it can pay dividends. It helps pupils gain a greater sense of commitment to
their role and to those of others in the group. The pupils could be asked to write
down these personal details for the hostel files. The information may be accompanied by a self-portrait, either in words or as a rough drawing. The details can also
be pinned up in the room, perhaps under a heading: 'The New Residents of
. . . Hostel.'

4 THE RESIDENTS ARRIVE AT THE HOSTEL

a *Whole group*
The teacher works in role as the Houseparent of a new hostel which will provide temporary accommodation for young people who have run away from home. They have been referred to the hostel by an agency and may be able to stay for the next two or three months before moving on to more permanent accommodation. They are fortunate to be there. Although the facilities are very basic and they will need to share bedrooms, there is a long waiting list for places of this kind. The stay will at least give them a breathing space.

The pupils represent the recently-arrived residents. The Houseparent shows them a plan of the hostel. As newcomers they are invited to ask questions about the layout of the hostel and the facilities available. These are very basic.

The Houseparent projects a sympathetic attitude but reminds them that they will all have to live together for a while and that certain rules are going to be necessary. Later on he will ask for their suggestions as to how things should be run. They might like to discuss their ideas with others but first of all they probably need to find out a little bit more about the people they will be living with for the next few months.

b *In pairs*
In pairs, the residents tell each other the reasons why they have decided to leave home and why they do not want to return. After a suitable period the individuals in each pair move on to somebody else. In this way it will be possible for pupils to find out about a number of their co-residents in a relatively short period of time.

Narrative link
The teacher can narrate the pupils into the next phase of the work.

'Towards the end of the morning, the new residents gathered together once again to talk to the Houseparent. They knew each other a little better now and while they were waiting for him to begin they sat with one or two of their new friends and talked about the kind of rules they thought would be necessary for the smooth running of the hostel.'

c *Whole group*
The teacher (in role) hopes that they will be patient while he checks some details for the hostel records. He needs to know:
— each person's name and home address
— members of family still living at that address
— reason for leaving home
The residents are asked to volunteer this personal information which is written up by the Houseparent or checked off against details already listed in a folder or register.

d   The discussion should really provide for a mixture of teacher/pupil interests. It is possible for the Houseparent to say that certain rules have been decided on in advance (by the Management Committee?) but many others are still left open to debate. The amount and nature of the responsibility given to the pupils in this matter will depend on the individual teacher and class, though the purpose of this activity is to set up a situation in which the pupils will be engaged in the processes of decision-making. In the interests of both authenticity and teacher control, it is useful to reserve the right to say, 'Oh, I'm sorry, that particular point has already been decided on, though, of course, decisions can always be changed later if things don't work out as planned.'

e   The written task may present a less threatening proposition for some pupils who would find it difficult to make an individual verbal commitment. Teachers will need to assess which of the two is most suitable for the particular group they are working with.

Another alternative is for the pupils to work in pairs (two room-mates?) and share these confidences with each other in private.

f   The pupils may need to be reminded that the accommodation on offer is likely to be very basic. How will they set about making it more comfortable and more attractive? Since the room will be shared with maybe two or three others, what measures will they take to obtain some degree of privacy? Will the occupants make any rules about the use of the room? What problems might arise? Pupils could be asked to produce individual plans of how they see the room and share their contributions with others in order to arrive at some agreement.

5*a*   The tableaux can be used as a starting-point for small-group improvisations which need not be shown to others.

The use of a caption card to describe each 'photograph' might be a useful device in introducing the content of the tableaux and linking them together in sequence.

d *Whole group: further work*
The residents are to be given some responsibility for drawing up the hostel rules.

They are invited to suggest the kind of rules they think would be appropriate and to name the sanctions to be applied if these are broken.

The rules can be listed on a large sheet of paper and could be dealt with under different headings. For example, those relating to practical, everyday activities involved in the smooth-running of a household, those relating to leisure activities, those relating to personal responsibilities etc.

e *Individual work*
At the end of their first day in the hostel each resident pauses to consider her situation.

The pupils sit alone in different parts of the room. Each pupil is asked either to speak or write her thoughts on
— the good things about their present situation
— the *one* thing that they miss most about their home, that which they rarely admit to themselves, let alone outsiders
The teacher can pose questions which help pupils to elaborate on their individual statements. For example, why did that *one* thing mean so much to you? What happened to change the situation?

If the work has been given as a written task (for example, as a letter or a diary entry) pupils could be asked to read the results to the rest of the class.

f *Individual further work*
Working in pairs or in small groups, the pupils draw a plan of their shared bedroom. There will be very little furniture, perhaps just a bed, a small cupboard and a chair for each person, but the residents are encouraged to arrange the room as they would like it. Do they have any personal items that will help to make the room theirs?

5 LIFE IN THE HOSTEL

a *Group work*
In groups, pupils prepare a 'dossier of photographs' showing some aspects of life in the hostel. Each group presents two or three tableaux which illustrate some of these features.
They could be shown in sequence as the record of a typical day. The groups will need to work out ways of linking the photographs together.

b *Further group work*
In groups, pupils devise a number of scenes showing an incident in which one of the hostel rules is broken.

In their planning they may need to consider:

c   Selection should be urged not on quality of performance but on what the scene yields that will be most interesting for group follow-up.

The teacher's task here is to support and focus the discussion but to leave as much as possible to the pupils themselves. If the class is competent at handling the situation, he may even absent himself altogether by going off to deal with some 'pressing business' in another part of the hostel. Part of this discussion may be concerned with asking the residents to think back to the way that problems were dealt with when they were living at home.

d   This kind of problem-sharing could also form the basis of small-group or pair-work activities.

e   These activities should be structured into the topic where appropriate. They do not have to be tackled in sequence. Each one can be repeated so that the pupils have a chance to take on both roles.

How many individuals are actually involved in breaking the rule?
Do the others present try to prevent it?
How is the incident discovered and by whom?
Do friends try to conceal the facts in order to protect those concerned?
Was the whole thing an accident or done quite deliberately?

The observers are invited to comment on the motives of the characters involved, on their blamelessness or otherwise and on the possible consequences that their action may have for the rest of the residents.

c *Whole group*
The pupils select one of the incidents shown for further enquiry. This will form the basis for a piece of drama involving the whole group.

The Houseparent summons the residents to his office. Those involved in the incident wait 'outside' for the moment. He explains that one of the hostel rules has been broken. He knows the people concerned and has asked them to come and talk to him. As an experiment, he has invited the other residents along so that they can see how such matters are dealt with. Maybe they would like to give their own opinions and advise him what is to be done. He reminds them that certain punishments were agreed on when the rules were drawn up. Should they be applied in this case?

The 'rule-breakers' are invited in to give their version of events. The residents ask questions and come to a decision as to whether the agreed sanctions should be applied.

d *Whole group*
Other aspects of the community's concern could also be dealt with in this way. Personal problems can be shared with the rest of the group at a full meeting of all the residents at which they give advice and support.

e *In pairs*
The following tasks can be used as a way of reintroducing the material after a break and of linking together different sections of the work. They also provide an opportunity for the pupils to look at the hostel and its residents from another perspective.

i   A is a resident of the hostel; B is a stranger whom A has met in a café. B asks about life in the hostel.
ii A lives opposite the hostel; B is a resident. They meet one day in the street and get involved in an argument in which A voices a list of criticisms about the hostel and its inhabitants.
iii The resident, A, is visited by a friend from home, B. Is it possible for B to persuade A to return?

f   If the teacher works in role here it will allow him to put the preparation of the plays into the broader context of hostel life. He can intervene as Houseparent, making suggestions and acting as organizer of the various tasks involved.

The pupils could be asked to work on a play which will help them to look back at some of the events of the drama and the roles they have played within it.

Many of the tasks listed here will cater for those pupils who do not want to take part in the performances.

6   The teacher takes on a role as the representative of the funding body (for example, a charitable trust, the local council etc.). Some of the pupils may wish to take on similar roles and sit with him to face the protesters. He is happy to listen to personal statements from the floor and is interested to know what happened to those present when they left the hostel at the end of their short stay.

Some associated written activities might be:
— making posters to publicize their cause.
— writing letters to other funding bodies, local MPs, the local newspaper.
— publishing a book through a local community printing press; each ex-resident contributes a personal reminiscence about life in the hostel.

iv   In a dream, hostel resident A speaks to parent B. During the conversation A and B talk of the good times that they once had together. B says that things could be like that again. A disagrees.

v   A has been in the hostel for over two months. B has just arrived and is not sure about staying. A points out the advantages.

vi   Two residents make plans for the future. They talk of the kind of place they would like to get (a flat, bedsit, long-term hostel accommodation?) Maybe they decide to share. How will they start looking? What work will they try to get? Do they already have social security payments? How will they organize their finances?

vii   A suddenly decides to leave the hostel and return home. How is the houseparent, B, told of this decision?

f   *Small groups*

Working in small groups, the residents prepare a number of short plays which they will present as part of an evening's entertainment at the hostel. The theme is 'Leaving Home'. The plays can have a happy ending, if this is what the group wants. As part of their preparation, pupils may also take on such tasks as:

— making costumes and properties.
— designing posters and programmes.
— setting up the performance and audience area.
— working out the running order of the plays.
— printing invitations to invited guests (the helpers from the agency for homeless young people?).

The houseparent is the chief guest. Other members of the audience will consist of those residents whose play has already been performed and those who are waiting for their turn.

6   THE HOSTEL UNDER THREAT

Whole group

It is five years later. The hostel may have to close because one of the funding bodies has decided to withdraw its support. Some of the former residents turn up at a meeting called to oppose the closure. They put their case to a representative of the organization concerned and argue that the hostel should be allowed to remain in business. They explain how it has helped them and many others in a similar situation. They say why they feel such places to be essential.

Do the ex-residents manage to bring about any change in the attitude of the person(s) from the funding body?

If not, how will the campaign be continued?

How will their cause be publicized?

Whose help do they need to enlist?

3 *The Lost Valley*

One of the principal features of this material lies in the opportunities it provides for dramatic play. Pupils are invited to reconstruct the life and work of a primitive society and participate in tasks related to shelter-building, hunting or gathering, preparing defences and organizing tribal celebrations. They will be asked to decide on the nature of the environment, the structure of the society and its laws, the division of labour and the technology available to them. The features of that society will largely be determined by the pupils' choices, and teachers should not be too concerned to relate it to one particular culture, location or period of historical development.

The work develops from a present-day starting-point in which a team of explorers prepares to re-create the life-style of a primitive tribe. The strategy allows the children to plan some of the things that will and will not be available to them in that situation, but they do this as part of the drama. The 'explorer' role can become redundant once the work is well established, and pupils may consequently decide to drop the pretence of the experiment, concentrating instead on their roles as members of the civilization they have created.

The work allows for a variety of approaches, including movement and dance, and should provide ample opportunity for related activities in art and literature.

SOURCE MATERIAL

The tribe travelled light. They were mainly naked but all of them were painted with white and black and red and yellow ochre. . . . The babies and small children were carried by the women on their backs in slings or bags made of animal skins and some of them wore mantles and lion bands of skin and had pouches and belts of leather. The men had stone-pointed spears and carried sharpened flints in their hands.

There was no Old Man who was lord and master of this particular crowd. Weeks ago the Old Man had been charged and trampled to a jelly by a great bull in the swamp far away. Then two of the girls had been waylaid and carried off by the young men of another larger tribe. It was because of these losses that this remnant was now seeking new hunting grounds.

. . . Before them stretched a great valley ridged with transverse purple hills over which the April cloud shadows chased one another. Pinewoods and black heather showed where these hills became sandy and the valleys were full of brown brush wood and down their undrained troughs ran a bright green band of peaty swamps and long pools of weedy water. In the valley thickets many beasts lurked unseen and where the winding streams had cut into the soil there were cliffs and caves. Far away along the northern slopes of the ridge that were now revealed, the wild ponies were to be seen grazing.

H. G. Wells, *The Grisly Folk*

At the end of another valley vegetation changed once more and we entered the gloom of the high mountain rain forest. The trees towered overhead now. The long straight trunks, some of which I estimated to be sixty feet high, rose into the enveloping cloud. I strode over to one . . . and tapped the trunk the way a landlubber knocks the wood of a boat to see how solid the vessel is. The tree was at least four feet across, smooth and utterly immoveable. And yet I knew for all its apparent strength it was as vulnerable as a sunflower in the wind. Such trees can easily topple.

Tony Morrison, *The Andes*

Finding it hopeless to push my way through the wood, I followed the course of a mountain torrent. At first, from the water falls and number of dead trees, I could hardly crawl along; but the bed of the stream soon became a little more open, from the floods having swept the sides. I continued slowly to advance for an hour along the broken and rocky banks, and was amply rewarded by the grandeur of the scene. The gloomy depth of the ravine well accorded with the universal signs of violence. On every side were lying irregular masses of rock and torn-up trees; other trees, though still erect, were decayed to the heart and ready to fall. The entangled mass of the thriving and the fallen reminded me of the forests within the tropics – yet there was a difference: for in these still solitudes, Death, instead of Life, seemed the predominant spirit.

Charles Darwin, *The Voyage of the* Beagle

The jungle was wide and full of twitterings, rustlings, murmurs, and sighs.
    Suddenly it all ceased, as if someone had shut a door.
    Silence.
    A sound of thunder.
    Out of the mist, one hundred yards away, came Tyrannosaurus Rex.
    'Jesus God', whispered Eckels.
    'Sh!'
    It came on great oiled, resilient, striding legs. It towered thirty feet above half of the trees, a great evil god, folding its delicate watchmakers' claws close to its oily reptilian chest. Each lower leg was a piston, a thousand pounds of white bone, sunk in thick ropes of muscle, sheathed over in a gleam of pebbled skin like the mail of a terrible warrior. Each thigh was a ton of meat, ivory, and steel mesh. And from the great breathing cage of the upper body those two delicate arms dangled out front, arms with hands which might pick up and examine men like toys, while the snake neck coiled. And the head itself, a ton of

sculptured stone, lifted easily upon the sky. Its mouth gaped, exposing a fence of teeth like daggers. Its eyes rolled, ostrich eggs, empty of all expression save hunger. It closed its mouth in a death grin. It ran, its pelvic bones crushing aside trees and bushes, its taloned feet clawing damp earth, leaving prints six inches deep wherever it settled its weight. It ran with a gliding ballet step, far too poised and balanced for its ten tons. It moved into a sunlight arena warily, its beautiful reptile hands feeling the air.

'My God!' Eckels twiched his mouth. 'It could reach up and grab the moon' . . . The Thunder Lizard raised itself. Its armoured flesh glittered like a thousand green coins. The coins, crusted with slime, steamed. In the slime, tiny insects wriggled, so that the entire body seems to twitch and undulate, even while the monster itself did not move. It exhaled. The stink of raw flesh blew down the wilderness.

Ray Bradbury, *A Sound of Thunder*

Faced with the modern world, many Indians have lost confidence in their own traditions. Once the forest has been chopped down, they have no way of making their own living. Instead, many Indians have turned to begging along the new roads, or in the nearby towns, in order to stay alive.

'We have the right to live in our land here. . . . We are the true Brazilians, not the whites. The whites came to fill up this land, to put an end to us. This is what they want.' (Tsererobo. Shavante chief. 1978)

Paul Henley, *Amazon Indians*

We aborigines like to live the quiet way. We like to go hunting, to sleep in the bush and listen to the birds singing, the animals crying, stomping their feet on the salt plains . . . now we don't have those things. There's the noise of bulldozers and cars and aeroplanes. (Mrs Joyce Hall, North Queensland Land Council)

Virginia Luling, *Aborigines*

FURTHER READING

Darwin, Charles, *The Voyage of the* Beagle, Everyman's Library, J. M. Dent, 1959

Henley, Paul, *Amazon Indians*, Macdonald Educational, 1980

Hugh-Jones, Stephen, *Amazon Indians*, The Archer Press, 1978

Jones, E. H., Hayhoe, M., and Jones, B., (eds.), *Pre-history and Early Man*, Routledge & Kegan Paul, 1969

Luling, Virginia, *Aborigines*, Macdonald Educational, 1979

Morrison, Tony, *The Andes*, Time Life Books, 1975

Turnbull, Colin, *The Forest People*, Chatto & Windus, 1972

TEACHING NOTES

The strategies outlined here were designed to meet the demands of single-period lessons. Some of them can be used to provide the material for an entire lesson, others will be of use in reintroducing the topic after a week's gap, moving the drama on or rounding off a particular phase of the work. In practice, each of the structures helped the children in this particular group to extend and deepen their commitment to the subject-matter over a period of several weeks.

1   The teacher chooses to approach the topic indirectly. He decides to set it within the context of an experiment designed to reconstruct a primitive way of life. This device will help him to find out what these pupils know about the subject-matter and to determine the kind of factual information he may subsequently need to provide that will be relevant to the needs of the drama. The work can begin without a lengthy exposition of facts. The 'experiment' convention allows the pupils a degree of ignorance; they don't have to possess an exhaustive knowledge of the subject.

  If the children are accustomed to the teacher working in role, they will have learned how to listen out for those clues that are given during this lengthy 'scene setting'.

The request for response invites pupils to formulate and pose relevant questions. With some classes it may be necessary for the teacher to give more obvious clues to the kind of issues that need to be raised. For example, 'I'm sure that many of you must be wondering just where this experiment will be taking place?' Alternatively, the teacher may ask the class to divide into small groups, with each group preparing the question they would like to ask.

  By directing the questions, the group members can have a larger stake in deciding upon the kind of environment they will enter and the conditions of the experiment. These will not be determined solely by the teacher.

  The question-and-answer session may form the major part of this short lesson. The teacher is prepared to devote time to this in-role discussion, since it stimulates the pupils' interest, builds up their belief in the experiment and prepares the ground

INTRODUCTORY LESSON

This theme was explored with a second-year mixed group working in the drama room for single periods of thirty-five minutes.

Objective
The lessons were planned as a contribution to the second-year integrated studies course. Through the drama the teacher wanted the group to examine the resourcefulness with which a primitive society adapts for survival.

Introduction
The teacher sits with the group on the floor of the drama room. He explains that the work he has planned will have links with the work they have been doing on primitive societies, but that he will start the drama in the present time.

Since he is not going to give them any further information they will have to listen very carefully to the clues he provides once he starts the work in role.

1   SETTING UP THE EXPERIMENT

Whole group
The teacher begins in this way:
'Welcome to the Scientific Research Institute. I am really pleased that you are the people who have finally been chosen for this experiment. Just think of it . . . for the next year we shall be living as the members of a primitive tribe, without many of the benefits of the twentieth century. We shall have to cope with unusual problems, I am sure, but the lessons learned may help us to find out more about such people and may be of benefit to us in our present-day situation.

'Now, you may have lots of questions you didn't have a chance to ask when you came to the interviews. I'll try to answer them for you here.'
The members of the experimental team begin to question him. They may ask:

> Where will this experiment take place?
> What is the environment like?
> Where will we live?
> What kind of food will there be?
> Will any communication with the outside world be allowed?
> What medical aid will be available?

At every available opportunity the teacher tries to hand over responsibility for answering these questions to other members of the group. He suggests that people may be present who have been chosen for precisely the kind of expertise that the enquiry indicates. For example, he asks if someone skilled in shelter-building can reply to a question about the kind of materials needed to construct a dwelling-place.

for subsequent drama work. If the pupils react unfavourably to this slow, 'building-up' approach, the teacher may switch to another activity early on. The initially slow pace may not be appropriate for those classes which need to be more *actively* engaged. Teachers who use this structure would be advised to select the strategies which seem most relevant to the needs of their particular groups.

The pupils in this case chose to adopt the term 'expedition'. The teacher, therefore, used this more frequently in place of his original 'experiment'.

2   Some children find it difficult to initiate and sustain pair work conversations of this kind. Teachers may need to ask the class to suggest the issues that might be raised during the course of the argument and instruct each pair to focus on one of these as a starting point for their dialogue. It will be necessary to monitor the development of the activity very carefully and step in to help those pairs that seem to be having difficulties, either by offering further points for discussion or by keeping the exercise short.

The paper is pinned on to a notice-board and two pupils write down the others' contributions. The activity provides a way of drawing together many of the points raised during the course of the lesson.

The second list may subsequently be used to remind pupils of the things that will or will not be available to them in coping with the difficulties they encounter. As the experiment progresses, these aids may become redundant.

3   The teacher is less concerned with the accuracy of the mimed demonstration

Where there are no volunteers, the teacher simply covers the fact by saying that those particular specialists were perhaps unable to attend today's meeting.

The pupils may want to know who will lead the 'expedition'. The teacher can agree to do so, at least in the early stages. Once the work is firmly established the group members may decide that this responsibility should be transferred to somebody else.

2   CONVINCING THE PUBLIC

In pairs
One of the most difficult of the early tasks will be to convince members of the public of the expedition's worth. The leader asks the team members to try out some ways in which they could 'sell' their experiment to other people.

In pairs, 'A' is a member of the general public, 'B' is a member of the team. A questions B as to the purpose of the project and its value to present-day society. The explorers may have to face considerable apathy or hostility.

The team leader asks the group to 'listen in' to some of the conversations and note the kind of defence now being put foward by the Bs in each pair. The roles are subsequently reversed.

The leader praises the members of the expedition for their spirited justification. It illustrates a determination to succeed.

Discussion
The teacher comments on the nature of the questions raised. They show an understanding of the kind of difficulties that would be faced by the members of an expedition like this. He explains that although they have not moved very far in terms of the drama, they have done some important work in laying the foundations for the future.

He asks the pupils to summarize the findings of the question-and-answer session. On a large sheet of paper they write down, 'What we already know about the place we are going to.' (The list includes details of the environment, seasonal variations in climate, geographical location and remoteness from the 'civilized' world.) They are invited to name *one small item* that they will each take with them and say why they think this will be of use in the struggle for survival. The objects are listed on a second sheet of paper: 'The only twentieth-century aids we will take with us.'

The lists will be kept for future reference.

[The first lesson was brought to a close at this point, but the following approaches were used to develop the theme in the sessions which followed.]

3   SHARING SKILLS

Each member of the group decides on the one special skill he would like to

than with the care and commitment which the pupils bring to the task. He reinforces the point that these skills will be of the utmost importance to the team's chances of survival.

If the class is prepared to continue with this exercise, the teacher can use it to raise questions about teaching and learning skills, the importance of accurate and precise instruction and the difficulties of communication.

4   Some classes may not be prepared to tolerate the delay in getting to grips with the central focus of the material — reconstructing the life-style of a primitive tribe. For such groups the making of a television programme may seem irrelevant.

What the strategy can do, however, is help to draw together what the children know about the project, clarify the resources that will be available and perhaps help them to articulate further their own belief in the worth of the expedition.

Some pupils may need to change roles and work as presenters, studio managers and interviewers. The 'studio' could be set up with separate areas for each of the items that will make up the programme. Considerable time may be needed to allow for the preparation of the various items and the organizational problems involved. The role of the programme producer would allow the teacher to oversee the whole operation, introduce 'deadlines', and provide an audience for the completed presentation.

5   Tape-recorders can be used for these interviews in pairs. The interview situations should be carefully set up, perhaps set in the press room of the Scientific Research Institute. The pressure provided by the use of a tape-recorder may help to maintain the formality of the situation, as may the use of a 'portapack' video machine, if available, to record the television programme.

6   'Photographs' and accompanying narrative links can be a useful and economical

contribute to the expedition. They write these on a sheet of paper listing all the skills available to the expedition.

a   *In pairs*
So that skills can be shared as widely as possible amongst all members of the team, the pupils teach their own brand of expertise to their partner. 'A' demonstrates a particular skill to 'B', and *vice versa*.

b   *Whole group*
In discussion, the group members share the difficulties involved in the teaching process. Some pupils may be prepared to demonstrate their new skills.

4   TELEVISION COVERAGE

Whole group
The team members make a programme which will attempt to explain the project to a wider public.

Pupils take responsibility for devising and presenting the programme, which is designed not only to justify the experiment but also shows the preparations that are being made, the kinds of expertise available to the project and the ways in which the members hope to reconstruct a primitive life-style.

The pupils will be involved in:
— preparing and explaining illustrative material, such as maps, drawings of the environment, shelters, and tools
— demonstrating how available skills will be put to use
— showing how they would cope with some of the problems that may occur
— setting up and conducting interviews in which expedition members are able to explain their commitment to the project, the attitudes of their family, the aspects of modern-day living they are most likely to miss.

5   A NEWSPAPER STORY

In pairs
'A' is a newspaper reporter, 'B' a member of the project team. The reporter is looking for a human-interest story, so the questions asked may be much more personal than those raised in the television programme.

What sort of background do the team members have? What are their ambitions? Have they ever been on an expedition like this before?

6   AN OFFICIAL PHOTOGRAPH

Whole group
The members of the expedition pose for an official photograph. They 'freeze' at

way of reintroducing material at the start of a new lesson, moving the work on from one dramatic activity to the next and rounding off the drama at the close of a lesson. A 'photo-strip', i.e. a number of 'photographs' linked together and dissolving from one to the next at a given signal, can provide an effective device in bridging a time-span or moving the action from one location to another.

The teacher may choose to select only those pupils whom he knows will be able to cope with this task. Alternatively, he may set it up as an exercise, in which the pupils speak the one word that is uppermost in their thoughts about the future.

7   The group should decide in advance on the physical nature of the new environment. The class whose work formed the starting-point for this material had earlier decided that its chosen environment would be a heavily forested valley; other groups may, of course, decide differently.

8   The pupils are given an opportunity to play at making their environment. The teacher may need to intervene and advise those groups who find this difficult. It may be necessary to forestall the kind of situations in which members of the party get killed by wild animals by curtailing the activity and narrating the group back to their central base. For example, 'Suddenly, for no apparent reason, the danger passed and the members of the expedition returned to safety.'
    The success of the sharing of their discoveries will depend on the pupils' willingness to pursue their dramatic playing; for some groups this type of mimed activity may prove embarrassing, or seem to be lacking in purpose. They may be unable to perform the tasks with any seriousness.

the moment when the 'photograph' is being taken. The teacher's narration can help to establish a setting for this activity, and also build the significance of the work that they undertake.

'The people in this photograph are taking an enormous step back into the past. They are about to re-create a way of life that has long since vanished. They know there may be many dangers. Their survival depends on their skills and on their ability to help each other. What thoughts are in their minds at this moment?'

The pupils are asked to voice their thoughts about the future, and speculate on the hazards and difficulties that lie ahead of them.

7   ARRIVAL IN THE VALLEY

Whole group
This strategy may follow quite naturally from the preceding one. Standing together as a group, the pupils close their eyes or turn away from the centre of the room. Once again, a narrative link is used to establish the situation.

'The preparations have been completed. The expedition members have said "good-bye" to their relatives, and have been brought by plane and overland transport to a remote part of the world where they will live for one year. The guides who have brought them to this place have now gone away and will return in twelve months' time.'

When the pupils open their eyes and turn to face the centre of the room they will be standing on the edge of the lost valley.

They may be asked to give their first impressions of what they see and state how this differs from their original conception. If they have decided to make some record of the expedition, they could be asked to draw a rough sketch showing one small aspect of the view that they can now see. The results are shared with the rest of the class.

8   EXPLORATION

Small groups
The pupils join up in small groups to make a tentative exploration of their environment. Each one may be made responsible for a specific task. For example, seeking out water and food, looking for suitable places to make a shelter, gathering wood, or identifying sources of danger.

The groups will return from their explorations at a given signal from the team leader. They will need to take care in marking out the route they have taken. With the completion of this activity the findings can be shared with others, either in discussion or through demonstration. The pupils may then need to work together in preparing a camp for the night, collecting and distributing food, and finding a source of water and suitable storage vessels.

The map work is best done on a very large sheet of paper. Groups mark out the territory they have been working in and illustrate some of its physical features.

10   A discussion of this kind may produce a very wide range of responses which can be used to open up an equally wide range of dramatic experiences. The teacher's ability to remain open to the pupils' initiatives will be a crucial factor in determining the subsequent development of the theme and it will be unwise to ignore the children's obvious interests by pressing on with his own pre-determined plan. For instance, if the meeting becomes most concerned with the existence of dangerous wild animals in the surrounding undergrowth, the teacher may find it extremely difficult to divert the pupils' interest. He would, therefore, be well advised to set up dramatic situations which capitalize on this. The whole group might be asked to design a trap to show how this would work in practice, perhaps as a carefully-controlled movement exercise. Smaller groups could be asked to show how they would hunt down such creatures without harm to themselves.

The allocation of responsibilities may provide a way of dealing with problems that affect actual class relationships. The teacher sets up parallel situations which help the pupils to look at the difficulties of operating in groups whilst the work is kept firmly within this fictional dramatic context.

11   The pupils may want to drop the convention of working as explorers engaged on a research project and pursue the drama from this point just as if they were members of a primitive tribe. In this case the teacher will need to revise some of the accompanying strategies, especially those in which, as part of the drama, the children are asked to draw upon their present day knowledge and expertise.

Pupils can be asked to keep a record of the experiences by making some simple stick-figure drawings depicting the incidents shown in the tableaux and scenes, for example, as drawn on pieces of bark or on slate.

The results of the exploration can be recorded on to one big map. Each group of pupils makes a record of the area they have explored.

9   THE FIRST EVENING

In pairs
In pairs, the members of the project team share their thoughts and fears about the coming year.

Is there anything they already miss about the life they have left behind? Is there any *one* thing which most frightens them about the future? What are they most looking forward to?

10   THE EVENING GATHERING

Whole group
The members come together to share food and drink and to discuss their first few hours in the valley.
The teacher leads the discussion in role. Areas of concern might include:

the ways in which the environment will pose problems for the team the most urgent tasks which now need to be done the appearance of particular problems which have not been anticipated

It may also prove valuable to discuss matters relating to:

the ways in which tasks will be defined and allocated the way in which responsibilities will be defined the process by which decisions will be taken

11   LIFE IN THE VALLEY

Small groups
The project team has been in the valley for several weeks.

In small groups, the pupils prepare a tableau which will show one aspect of life in this new environment. Each group should choose a different moment, perhaps working chronologically through a typical day. For example, one group shows the kind of work that is done at first light, and so on.

Alternatively, groups may choose to focus on an important event that has happened to these people in their time together.

The tableaux are shown to the other members of the class. They can then be 'brought to life' with accompanying dialogue or narration.

The scenes might also show an example of the ingenuity with which the team members have dealt with the problems they have encountered. How do they

12   The teacher may need to stress that the dangers have been overcome successfully. This exercise will help the team members to look back on what happened and draw up plans to prevent their reccurrence. If some pupils insist on 'dying' during the course of this activity, or at any other available opportunity, then the teacher is left with a number of choices. He may be able to use the 'death' as the starting-point for a piece of drama which looks at how the remaining members of the team deal with the loss of a colleague. He may need to explain that 'death' will remove pupils from any involvement in this part of the drama and that their main task would be to observe and record the events. If 'sickness' spreads through the group the teacher may present the class with certain options. If they all die then the experiment will have failed and so the work ends here; alternatively, the group members recover and the work goes on. Those who remove themselves from the drama by 'death' could subsequently be asked to take on other roles, for example, as members of another tribe or as the dead souls of a previous expedition who return to give advice, warning and assistance to the present group.

14*a* and *b*   The results of all these preparations can form part of an evening's

ensure their survival in a hostile environment having only the most primitive means at their disposal?

12   UNEXPECTED DANGERS

Small groups
The pupils prepare a number of scenes which show how the team members fared at moments of greatest danger. It may be that such dangers arise out of the most unexpected causes. They do not necessarily involve a physical threat. They could come from within the group itself.

In their planning, groups should be asked to consider:

> the kinds of danger that would most threaten the existence and success of the venture. In what ways would the explorers' survival be most at risk?
> the moment when the threat becomes apparent and the ingenuity used to deal with it
> the type of preventative action taken
> the most frightening moment

13   REVIEWING THE DANGERS

Whole group
The scenes of dangers are shown to a gathering of the team members, as a reminder of the difficulties faced and overcome to date. The teacher sets up the meeting in role, introduces each of the scenes and leads the discussion, helping the pupils to focus on such questions as:

What lessons have been learned from these experiences?
How were the dangers overcome? Would twentieth-century aids have been of use in combating them?
Could such dangers arise again?
What precautionary measures need to be taken?
How responsible were members of the group in helping each other to combat the threat?

14   LEGENDS, RITUALS AND DANCES

Small groups
During their time in the valley the group have attempted to live as primitive peoples might have done. It what ways will their lives have been different? Is their language the same? Are their beliefs the same? What would primitive people have believed about the seasons, or the origin of the sun, moon and stars?

a   *Legends*
In small groups, the pupils are asked to invent some of the legends which may

gathering or be incorporated into a much grander occasion, for example, a celebration of the first six months in the valley. Each group has a dual role to play here working both as performers of their own piece and as members of the audience at the festival or gathering. The teacher operates as the organizer of the event, setting each offering within the overall framework, though he may ask the pupils to consider:

how they will arrange the space in which the performances are to be presented;
the way in which the individual performances will be linked together;
the way in which people will be asked to arrive at the celebratory gathering;
the kind of welcome they will each be given.

The teacher will be creating a dramatic context for the theatrical presentations.

Each group will be engaged in preparing and setting up a piece of drama that will involve the rest of their classmates.

c   This task is included as suitable only for these classes who have a certain degree of movement experience since it demands considerable sensitivity and control.
   The work requires a large area of unrestricted space. It may generate high levels of noise and activity and is best avoided where there are any discipline problems, where other classes are likely to be disturbed, or where the class is unable to work within and abide by the conventions of slow-motion activity.

15   If this topic is reached after a break, a reminder of the time passed together can be introduced by this exercise. The teacher and group sit in a circle. Each person contributes one memory of their time together so far: 'I remember the time when. . . .'

help primitive people to explain the existence of certain natural phenomena. There are various ways in which these may be presented:

> as a dance drama or as a piece of mime
> in a series of tableaux with linking passages of narration
> as a collection of scenes with dialogue
> in verse or song
> as a story (with different groups responsible for telling different parts)

b   *Ritual*

Similarly, the class may be asked to consider the importance of ritual in the lives of primitive (and modern) peoples. In small groups, pupils prepare a ritual which could be used for:

> dealing with sickness
> celebrating success in battle or hunting
> marking Midsummer or Midwinter
> honouring births, adulthood, marriages, deaths

When each group has planned the ritual they should attempt to involve the rest of the group so that the whole class takes an active part. The teacher introduces each ritual with a narrative link or one of the groups sets the scene.

c   *Dance*

At one time the valley may have been inhabited by dinosaurs or similar creatures. The people of the valley prepare a dance which celebrates these past inhabitants. This, too, could be presented at a festival or gathering.

Working in small groups, the children combine to represent, in movement, a creature with the power, size and ferocity of a dinosaur. The work should not attempt to be realistic. It is the strength of the animal they will be trying to suggest.

What would happen if such creatures should meet? *In slow motion*, the groups prepare a movement sequence which shows what happens if a battle occurred between two or more of these giants. Sound effects or a musical accompaniment can be provided by members of the group or those not involved in the movement activity itself.

15   ELECTING A LEADER

Whole group

The members of the project team have been living and working together for several months. They have shared a large number of experiences.

The team leader calls the group together for the meeting and announces this his original plan was to relinquish leadership of the group once the experiment was

Although the election of a new leader is designed to give rise to in-role discussion about the qualities and responsibilities of leadership, a hand-over should only be considered if the teacher feels comfortable relinquishing the authority role and if classes will be able to cope with him doing so. The transfer of the leadership is unlikely to prove a very satisfactory strategy if pupils lack the ability to co-operate effectively without the teacher's constant intervention. In such cases it would only be worth attempting as a way of initiating discussion about the importance of group co-operation and the difficulties involved in reaching corporate decisions.

16*a*   If the pupils have previously decided to relinquish their role as 'explorers' and have developed the drama as the members of a primitive society, then the nature of this discussion will, of course, take on a slightly different flavour.

b   It is not necessary to share these meetings with the group, but the teacher

firmly established. The time now seems right to do so. The group is asked to elect a new leader in his place, or perhaps devise alternative systems in which leadership is shared amongst several members of the group, or in which each member has equal responsibility.

Does the group want one person to be in charge or should this responsibility
   be divided?
What qualifications will the group members look for in their leader(s)?
Have these qualifications been proven in their life together over the past few
   months? In what ways?
Are these qualities more appropriate to twentieth-century life-style, or the
   conditions under which they now find themselves?
How will the election be carried out?

If there is to be an election, then its conduct and the announcement of results should be handled with great formality. Each member of the group may be required to make a promise of some kind to the new leader, and *vice versa*.

16   MEETING ANOTHER TRIBE

a   *Whole group*
This section may be introduced with a narrative link:
'One day, as the weather was growing colder, some members of the group were hunting on the edges of the valey. Because food was getting scarce, they had travelled much further than they usually did. In the distance, they suddenly saw smoke. They cautiously drew nearer until they realized that the smoke was rising from a clearing bordered by dwellings. They had wandered into the territory of what seemed to be a tribe of primitive people.'
   At this point, it may be wise to ask the group whether those members who saw the tribe would like to describe them. Alternatively, the news might be brought to the camp by individuals acting as look-outs.

What did the tribespeople look like?
In what ways were they different from modern people?
What were they doing?
Did they look dangerous?

The presence of another tribe so close to the valley may present problems for the group. What should they do? Is it safe to continue the experiment? Should they try to make contact with the people they have seen?

b   *In pairs*
'A' and 'B' discuss what they think should be done. One of the partners may be

should try to monitor what is going on and discourage caricature or signs of physical aggression. It may be helpful to formalize the meetings and to build in some controls by asking the partners to face each other across a 'clearing', for example, two lines chalked on the floor. At this first meeting no closer contact is made. If any pairs are working with particular effectiveness and belief, it may be possible for the rest of the group to 'eavesdrop' on the meeting.

17   The teacher may need to leave the organization and direction of this meeting to the newly-elected leader.

18a   Some members of the group may need to change roles for this activity and represent people from the neighbouring tribe. If pupils seem sufficiently interested the work could be developed to look more closely at the meeting of the two societies. What can one learn from the other and *vice versa*? Will such a meeting harm the culture of the primitive tribe? What benefits might be gained by either group?

   For the sake of the drama, a more fruitful dialogue is likely to result if the pupils agree to the convention that both parties communicate in a common language.

b   A small blanket or covering could be used to signify the presence of the baby within this community. The teacher shows it to the assembled gathering and suggests that the baby itself is safe in one of the shelters.

   The teacher's contributions to this discussion should press the group towards

concerned to leave well alone, to withdraw from the valley; the other may press for further exploration.

A and B then act out an imaginary meeting between one of the project team and one of the tribespeople. They may want to attempt several versions of the same encounter, perhaps using different approaches.

> What happens when they meet?
> Can they communicate?
> What have they in common?
> How will A signal friendship to the member of the tribe, B?

17   THE EVENING MEETING

Whole group
The members of the project team set up their usual evening gathering in order to decide what is to be done about their newly-discovered neighbours. Is it safe to stay? What are the implications of a meeting between the two groups? How would such a meeting be arranged? What forms of communication would be used? What might either group gain from such a meeting?

18   SETTING A PROBLEM

a   *Whole group*
This can be introduced with a narrative link or be related by the teacher in the first person. It presents a specific problem for the group to consider.
'During the day, one of the group was fishing in the river and noticed that there was something floating in the water. It seemed to be a rough basket. The group member reached into the water and pulled it out. Lying in the basket was a baby. It obviously belonged to the tribe further up the river.'

At this point, discussion might be focused on such considerations as:

> How did the baby come to be in the river?
> If it was an accident, how can the group bring the baby safely back to the
>   tribe without revealing their own presence?
> If it was deliberate, why have the tribe done this?
> What responsibility does the group have towards the baby?

What is to be done?

b   *Small groups*
Each group is asked to choose one of the decisions that could be made in relation to the newly-discovered child. They prepare and show a scene which demonstrates the results of their decision.

Alternatively, the teacher can represent a member of the newly-discovered

recognizing the consequences of any decision taken.

20*a*   The evidence can be drawn on to individual sheets of paper with each pupil explaining the significance of the selection to the rest of the group.

A final 'photograph' of the team members preparing to leave the valley might prove a useful device for signalling the end of the experiment.

b   The explorers could also be asked to contribute articles to a range of newspapers and magazines covering a number of specialist fields, for example, historical, anthropological, scientific, ecological, sociological, geographical, etc. Diaries and personal accounts also may be prepared for publication.

tribe. He comes to the explorers' camp. Is he hostile, suspicious, curious or friendly? What does he want to know? How do the members of the team explain who they are and what they are doing there? Does he see them as a threat to the continued existence of his people? It should be possible for the role to present a number of challenges which may help the pupils to explain and justify their presence.

20   THE RETURN

a   *Whole group*
It is time for the group to return to the present. The experiment is at an end. At a final gathering the explorers discuss their year in the valley.

> What have they learned in this time?
> Will this knowledge be useful to other people?
> How could it be utilized?
> What were the best and worst moments of their time together?
> Is there to be a leave-taking of the neighbouring society?
> Will the rest of the world be told of that tribe's existence or should the people
>   be allowed to remain as they are?

Each member of the team describes the single piece of evidence they will take back with them as a reminder of their year in the valley.

b   *Whole group*
On their return, the explorers are invited, once again, to a television studio. They prepare a programme which will share the results of their experiment with the wider public.

> What were the major problems encountered?
> How were these overcome?
> Has the experiment been a success? In what ways?
> What benefits have they brought back?
> Would they do it again?
> What were the most difficult decisions they had to take?
> Did they meet any other people?

4 Victorians

INTRODUCTION

This theme will offer considerable challenge. It will make demands on the ability of pupils to enter into the thoughts, feelings and attitudes of people distanced from them in time and circumstance.

Pupils should be able to draw on any existing knowledge of Victorian life to help them experience something of what it was like to be poor and helpless in a divided society. Exploring this theme may help them to understand how change and reform can come about in response to pressures from within society.

In this structure the pupils may be required to change roles during the different activities. They may become poor children, workhouse inmates, charitable commissioners, members of a wealthy and privileged family. If they are not accustomed to altering their roles in the drama they may find these changes difficult, but approaching the theme from a variety of viewpoints should enrich their understanding and develop their competence in adopting a number of roles within a piece of work.

Because of the nature of the theme, considerable formality may be appropriate at times during the structure, for example, in setting up the courtroom or applying to the charitable commissioners. This formality may further challenge the pupils. The theme is also likely to motivate further research and may lead to valuable written and art tasks.

SOURCE MATERIAL

In the 1880s, when Dr Barnardo was a teacher at a Ragged School in London's East End, he discovered almost by accident that one of his pupils, an urchin called Jim Jarvis, had neither parents nor home. Jim's mother had been dead for years, and he could not remember his father. He was only 10 years old but he had no one to take care of him and was completely destitute. When his mother died he had been put in a workhouse but had run away. He was forced to sleep out of doors, and for this offence had been sent to prison. He slept in gutters, under tarpaulins in the market, in barrels, or in any other place which would provide some shelter. The previous night he had slept in a haycart, which had been warm and comfortable compared with his other resting places.

Barnardo could hardly believe such poverty existed. He enquired if there were any other homeless and friendless orphans in London. Jim Jarvis told him that hundreds of children lived in these conditions, and agreed to show Dr Barnardo their hiding places. Jim Jarvis led him through the dark streets and dirty alleyways until they reached Petticoat Lane. Here, on the roof of an old clothes shop, Barnardo found a number of children huddled together, ragged and half-starved, but asleep in the cold.

Chimney-sweeps
Their number was increased by parish apprentices, the parishes usually adopting that mode as the cheapest and easiest way of freeing themselves from a part of the burden of juvenile pauperism. The climbing boys, but more especially the unfortunate parish apprentices, were almost always cruelly used, starved, beaten and over-worked by their masters, and treated as outcasts by all with whom they came into contact.

Henry Mayhew, *London Labour and the London Poor*

Victorian Towns
A horde of ragged women and children swarm about, as filthy as the swine that thrive on the garbage heaps and in the puddles. . . . The race that lives in these ruinous cottages behind broken windows mended with oilskin . . . or in dark wet cellars in measureless stench and filth . . . must really have reached the lowest stage of humanity.

Friedrich Engels, *Condition of the Working Class in England*

Mud larks
Not one of them was over twelve years of age, and many of them were but six. Some carried baskets filled with the produce of their morning's work, and others old tin kettles with iron handles. Some had old hats filled with the bones and coals they had picked up; and others more needy still, had actually taken the caps from their own heads and filled them with what they happened to find. The muddy slush was dripping from their clothes and utensils, and forming a puddle where they stood. There did not appear to be among the group as many filthy cotton rags to their backs as when stitched together would have been sufficient to form the material of one shirt. There were the remnants of one or two jackets among them, but so begrimed and tattered that it would have been difficult to have determined either the original material or make of the garment.

Henry Mayhew

Tom, the chimney-sweep
'He lived in a great town in the North Country, where there were plenty of chimneys to sweep and plenty of money for Tom to earn and his master to spend. He could not read or write and did not care to do either; and he had never washed himself for there was no water

up the court where he lived. He had never been taught to say his prayers. He cried half his time and laughed the other half. He cried when he had to climb the dark flues, rubbing his poor knees and elbows raw; and when the soot got into his eyes, which it did every day in the week; and when his master beat him, which he did every day in the week likewise.'

Charles Kingsley, The Water Babies

The collier's family

I entered several houses, which were miserably furnished, and agreed with the general aspect of the exterior. The first I entered was occupied by a collier and his family, consisting of a wife and six children; the furniture of this house, that is, bed, bedding, chairs, tables, kitchen utensils, etc, if put up to the hammer, might probably have realised 10s. A few days previously to my visit, the father and the eldest son, who worked in the coal pits, and were the support of the family, had both been seriously burned by an explosion of gas, or as they called it, 'fire-damp', in the pit, and were both disabled. The father expected soon to be able to resume his work, but the son was so dreadfully burned on the face, head and arms, that it was thought at one time that he would lose his sight; however, when I called, he had hopes that would not be the case; but it was thought he would not be able to work for three months.

William Dodd, Wigan, 1841

A pit-girl from Halifax

'My father has been dead about a year; my mother is living and has ten children, five lads and five lasses; the oldest is about thirty, the youngest is four; three lasses go to mill; all the lads are colliers; one lives at home and does nothing; mother does nought but look after home.

I never go to day-school; I go to Sunday-school, but I cannot read or write; I go to pit at five o'clock in the morning and come out at five in the evening; I get my breakfast of porridge and milk first; I take my dinner with me, a cake, and eat it as I go; I do not stop or rest any time for the purpose; I get nothing else until I get home, and then have potatoes and meat, not every day meat. I work in the clothes I have now got on, trousers and ragged jacket; the bald place upon my head is made by thrusting the corves; my legs have never swelled, but sisters' did when they went to mill.'

From the first report of the commission on the employment of children, 1842

FURTHER READING

Dickens, Charles, *Oliver Twist*, Everyman's Library, J. M. Dent, 1963

Hugget, Frank E., *Factory Life and Work*, Harrap, 1973

Kelsall, Freda, *How We Used to Live in Victorian Times*, Macdonald Educational, 1978,

Kingsley, Charles, *The Water Babies*, Allen & Unwin, 1978, first published 1863

Mayhew, Henry, *London Street Life*, ed. Raymond O'Malley, Chatto and Windus, 1966

Palmer, Roy, *Poverty Knock*, Cambridge University Press, 1974

Pollard, Michael, *The Victorians*, Heinemann Educational Books, 1978

Unstead, R. J., *A Century of Change*, A. & C. Black, 1963

Wymer, Norman, *Dr Barnardo*, Longman, 1962.

TEACHING NOTES

This introductory discussion was very brief. The teacher needs to judge carefully whether there is much to be gained by a lengthy introductory discussion and whether the group can sustain it. This class had some background knowledge of the period from their reading, but it would be possible to begin in the same way with groups who have only a sketchy idea of conditions at the time.

1   At this early point in the work commitment and belief will be limited. The teacher points out the difficulty of the task on which they are engaged. It is necessary to try to imagine that they are cold and hungry, lying in a dark London street, when in fact they are in a warm, bright school hall.

Narration by the teacher is a useful device to establish that the drama has begun, and to create atmosphere.

The teacher is in role as a caring, responsible adult – a role which may not be too different from her real stance as teacher. The rest of the group may be able to hear only part of this dialogue, but their curiosity should act as a control.

This is a crucial moment for the teacher. She is asking a great deal of one girl. In persuading the rest of the group to come to the 'house', this one girl has the responsibility of maintaining the make-believe, which has only just begun, and of supporting the rest of the group in their roles.
   The 'house' is represented by a circle of chairs.

INTRODUCTORY LESSON

This lesson took place with a class of thirty second-year girls in a large school hall. Each lesson was a fifty-minute session.

Objective

To introduce a new way of working in drama to the group who were more accustomed to reading and presenting plays. A second objective was to use drama to complement the reading which the group had been doing in English lessons (*Oliver Twist*).

Introduction

The teacher spends a few minutes talking with the group about what life might have been like in Victorian London. Their replies show some grasp of the atmosphere of the time, and an understanding of the conditions in which children might have lived in the London streets. The teacher asks the group whether they could imagine that *they* were those children. They agree to try.

1   THE CHILDREN OF THE STREETS

Individual work

The teacher asks each of the group to find somewhere in the hall that might represent the place in which they had spent the previous night. The pupils spread out and take up positions under chairs and in corners. At first there is some giggling, but after a few moments the class settles down.

Narrative link

Moving quietly about the hall, the teacher begins a piece of narration:
'It was Christmas Eve, in the year 1850, during the reign of Queen Victoria. The streets of London were cold, dark and silent. A figure was making its way homeward through the empty streets . . .'

Teacher in role

The teacher walks slowly round the hall, and stops suddenly beside a girl huddled under the piano. She is shocked to discover someone sleeping in the streets. Speaking so that the rest of the group can hear as much as possible of the conversation, she questions the girl. She is horrified to hear that there are many children in the same situation – she has only recently arrived in London and doesn't know about conditions there. She points out her house to the girl – 'the big house on the corner of the square' – and asks her to bring any other children who are sleeping on the streets with her to the house as soon as possible. She explains that she is not a wealthy woman, but that at least she can give them something to eat and shelter for the night.

2   If the teacher has inadvertently selected someone as her agent who is not accepted by the rest of the class, the drama may have to stop here.

The motions of entering the circle may cause some amusement and exaggerated play which breaks the mood that is gradually being created. The concern of the 'charitable lady' at their condition may help the pupils to work more seriously, as should the sensitive responses of the rest of the group.

The teacher tries to encourage every pupil to make some contribution.

As the members of the group begin to define their roles, the teacher's role also becomes less neutral. She begins to challenge individuals about their way of life, and to show not just concern but also some disapproval.

During this section of the work, the teacher is trying to encourage the responses of the class by creating the impression that *they* are the people with the information. *They* know what life is like on the streets, and she doesn't. Therefore she will accept what they say, although she may be incredulous or disapproving. The quality of the pupils' responses improve gradually during this session, until they begin to be able to look at the idea of Christmas from a totally new point of view.

3   This kind of work may be difficult for some pupils, but it offers them the opportunity of developing an individual response and becoming more deeply involved in a particular role.

2   DISCOVERIES ABOUT LIVING CONDITIONS

Whole group

The teacher returns to the circle of chairs, and waits for the girl to whom she has spoken to collect the others and bring them to her. Gradually, the pupils come into the circle. Some sit on chairs, while others huddle on the floor. One or two seem to be so weak and ill that they have to be helped into the 'house' (the circle of chairs) by their friends.

When the group is settled, the teacher, maintaining her attitude of concern, questions them closely about their life. Her questions focus on the following areas:

Where have they been sheltering?
When did they last eat?
How do they make a living?
Do any of them work?
Where are their mothers and fathers?
What happened to their families?

The replies are thoughtful, and the pupils are gradually feeling their way into appropriate roles and language. The teacher tries to follow up and develop the most fruitful responses, and her attitude becomes more noticeably Victorian. She is shocked by any suggestion of dishonesty, and by the children's apparent ignorance of religion. They seem to know nothing about the church, and though it is Christmas, they don't know what this means, or what is being celebrated. Some of the group point out that they have been refused entry to churches because they are poor and dirty. 'Church is only for rich people,' one girl says. The charitable lady tries to explain the meaning of Christmas to them. They are intrigued to hear that Jesus was also poor, and are very interested in the idea of presents.

The charitable lady gives the group some food and allows them to settle down for the night. She is rather disturbed by suggestions that some of the group are dishonest, and hopes that she can trust them. In the morning, she will have to consider what to do with them.

3   THE CHRISTMAS PRESENT

Individual work

Stepping out of role, the teacher asks the class to think of what they would most like in the world to have for a Christmas present. She explains that these children, who have so little, may not wish for conventional gifts. Slowly moving round the group, she touches each pupil in turn, and each speaks her thoughts aloud. Some wish for material things – clothes and food – while others wish for things which may help them make a living. One girl says that what she wants most in the world is a mother and father.

4   The primary task here is presented by the teacher as information gathering. Any facts which are gleaned from these scenes can be listed by the teacher on a blackboard.

The way in which the teacher chooses to develop the work will be determined by the interests of the group in the theme, and by their needs and capacities. There may be little point in continuing with the theme if the pupils' response seems likely to remain superficial and if their reactions in role are stereotyped.

5   The experience of the group in this part of the sequence is likely to be one of helplessness in the face of bureaucracy.

   If none of the group wishes to be a member of staff, it may still be possible for the teacher to represent the attitudes of the staff. If the teacher is working alone, the interviewing of new inmates may be a lengthy procedure. It may be wise to give the class some time to decide on the details of their lives, and maybe even to write them down before the work begins. Some of the class may decide to change roles and become different members of families, but it is possible for them to continue as the children of the previous section if these roles are beginning to develop.

   The arrangement of the space available will assist in creating the atmosphere of formality and discomfort which might accompany this scene. It will be important to

4   HARDSHIPS

Small groups

The teacher asks the class to work in groups of five or six. The task is to prepare and show a short scene which will tell the rest of the class something about the way they have been living. Some of these scenes show the children living by their wits, while others show the poverty and violence of the homes some of them once knew. The teacher's comments afterwards encourage the class to consider the children's relationship with each other, their attitudes to authority, and the ways in which they cope with the hardships of their lives.

[The first session ended at this point. The group had become increasingly absorbed in the work and were anxious to continue with the theme. For a teacher working in a similar way, there would now be a number of options. The choice of strategy would depend on her particular objectives for the class, and the needs and abilities of the group.

The drama might develop through an exploration of the life of the poor, and in particular of poor children, in Victorian times. This approach is likely to involve the class in research, and the activities described below could be enriched by selected reading – *Oliver Twist*, parts of *The Water Babies*, *Doctor Barnardo*. There should be an increase in understanding of the plight of the poor, and the gap that existed between rich and poor at this time. A second direction might be to examine the problems of improving the lot of the poor, and the difficulties of administering charity. In this structure, these approaches are presented as succeeding each other, but the teacher will have to judge whether it is appropriate to work through the entire sequence, or to select only some of the activities for the pupils. She must also be ready to follow the work in the direction which leads away from that described in the sequence, if this is where these pupils' interests lie, and if the direction seems a fruitful one for learning. In this case, the activities described in the structure may no longer be appropriate, but the strategies may easily be adapted by the teacher and used in a different context.]

5   THE WORKHOUSE

Whole group

If the chronology of the story has become important to the children, it should be possible to suggest that the charitable lady could not keep the children any longer and sent them to the workhouse. Alternatively, perhaps they returned to the streets, where they were found and brought to the workhouse.

Several members of the class may choose to be the staff of the workhouse for this part of the work. The teacher, in role as Superintendent or Warden of the place, can co-ordinate their efforts. The Warden and staff receive the new arrivals.

These will be formal proceedings, with the staff of the workhouse at tables and the new arrivals waiting their turn, perhaps on chairs or in a queue. Each person

create the distance between inmates and staff, and show this in the physical layout of the room. If chairs are used for inmates while they are waiting, these should be formally arranged in a square or row of chairs. The discipline of the workhouse is established by this formality.

A discussion following this section may be useful:

In what ways will their new life differ from their lives on the streets?
What does the class know about workhouses?
What further research will be necessary?

6a   In this 'bringing to life' of the tableaux, the teacher is on the outside of the work. Yet she must try to monitor what is happening in the groups. At what level of feeling are the groups working? Are they engaging in dramatic playing, which may be rambling and without depth, or are they managing to maintain appropriate roles and language?

Even if the children are 'playing' at this activity, it may be important to allow it to continue for a while. Although the work may appear superficial, it could be that the groups need this time to develop detail and to begin to believe in their predicament. The question of how long this activity should continue is further complicated by the fact that groups may be working in different ways, and at different levels.

b   This will probably be quite a brief exercise. Its function is to allow reflection on the previous section of the work.

7   These may be represented by a few members of the class who are prepared to change roles, or by a colleague, a student or someone from another class.

will be required to give an account of themselves – their names and age, their family connections, their possessions and resources, and the reasons which have led them to ask for official charity.

The staff will need to elicit these details from the inmates, and press for as full an account as possible. Their attitude to the new arrivals is likely to be at best indifferent, and may be harsh and unsympathetic.

After each person has been interviewed, their duties and the routine of life in the workhouse will be explained to them by the staff.

6 LIFE IN THE WORKHOUSE

a *Small groups*
Each small group prepares and shows a moment from a day in the workhouse – perhaps sleeping arrangements, work, meal-times, leisure. The result should be a series of tableaux, which can be co-ordinated by the teacher. After each one has been seen by the class, is it possible for the people in the tableau to answer questions from the rest of the group, while remaining in role?

What are they feeling now?
What is their clearest memory?
Have they any hope for the future?
Whom do they blame for the situation they are in?

After the tableaux have been shown, each group is asked to bring their tableau to life and live through part of the workhouse day. Each group will be working simultaneously, and there will be no need to share this part of the work with the rest of the class.

b *In pairs*
Each person should work with someone who has been in another group. Can they share what they feel about the workhouse?

What is the hardest thing to bear?
Is the life worse than it was on the streets?
Are there any good things about it?
Is there anything to look forward to?

---

7 THE VISIT

Whole group
The inmates are summoned together by the staff for an important announcement. The workhouse will be visited by one or more very important people – perhaps a magistrate, an inspector of workhouses, or a wealthy benefactor. The workhouse must be presented in the best possible light. If the inmates do not co-operate, their few existing privileges will be taken away.

8   Here, the sequence of incidents will need to be co-ordinated by the teacher.
    After these occurrences, the drama may take a new direction. If the visitors are
affected by what they have witnessed, they may wish to complain to the Warden.
What effect might this have on the lives of the inmates? An enquiry might be set up
into the running of the workhouse, and the inmates required to give evidence. The
group might wish to consider how a reformed workhouse should be run, and even
show it in action.

9a   Since the teacher's previous role may have been a strongly unsympathetic one,
it may be best to remain on the outside of this piece of the work, and leave
responsibility for the planning to the group. If pupils seem unable to plan or discuss
adequately in the drama, it is always possible to halt the work, and hold a class or
small-group discussion about the plight of the children, and their plans for the
escape. It may then be possible to return to the 'living through'meeting where they
plan the escape.
    The teacher has a stage-management function in co-ordinating this section, so
that the escape attempt begins as planned. It may be possible to introduce an
element of surprise or challenge to what the pupils have planned which will increase
the tension and may stretch their wits, for example, the unexpected arrival of the
Warden in the dormitories. It is in moments like these that the work is likely to
take an unexpected direction which the teacher must be prepared to follow if she is
truly to accept the children's contributions. If she is unable to decide how best to
organize what may be a crucial moment in the drama, it is always possible to 'mark
time' by introducing another activity, or to clarify the thoughts of the group by
stopping the drama to reflect on what has happened.

When the staff feel that the workhouse is ready for inspection, the visitors arrive. The teacher, still in role as the Warden, shows them round, and entertains them to tea. Is it possible for the inmates to make the visitors understand what life is like for them, without arousing the hostility of the Warden? Can they bridge the gulf between the visitors and themselves? The visitors may be indifferent to the inmates, or they may be horrified at their plight and wish to help them.

8   INCIDENT

Small groups
An incident occurs while the visitors are in the workhouse, which reveals to them the truth about the conditions there. Each group is asked to plan and show an incident which might help to change the visitors' minds in their favour. The visitors come to each group in turn and witness the incident.

> How do they interpret the incident?
> Can the staff explain it away?
> Do things turn out as the inmates had hoped?

9   ESCAPE

Narrative link:
'Conditions in the workhouse have become intolerable. Many of the young people there are determined to stand it no longer. It is late at night. They have crept from their beds, and meet together to plan their escape.'

a *Whole group*
The meeting is held in conditions of great secrecy. The group will be considering the following questions:

> What preparations can they make before the escape?
> How can they get out of the workhouse without being seen?
> Will they need to distract the Warden and staff in any way?
> Should they all stick together?
> Where is the safest place to go?

When the escape is thoroughly planned, the group should carry it through, perhaps from a starting-point provided by the teacher's narration. They must be prepared to cope with the unexpected. If anything happens during the escape attempt – if there is an accident or someone is injured – then the consequences must be faced, and worked through. Even if the escape is unsuccessful, an enquiry into the conduct of the workhouse might result, which could lead to better conditions for everyone. Alternatively, as a punishment, the regime might become even harsher.

b   A 'marking time' activity might be the dream of escape, as described opposite, but this time it is happening in *anticipation* the night before the escape is to take
place. Another way of allowing the teacher some thinking time is to adopt a
non-drama activity, perhaps the letter which the children leave for a friend who is
staying behind in the workhouse, or a poem describing the feelings of the workhouse inmates.

10   It is important for the teacher to judge the level of interests in the work
before proceeding with another section. It might not be appropriate to work
through both the Workhouse and the Chimney-sweep sections, unless the needs of
the group and the interest level suggest that both should be attempted.

a   It is important to differentiate this role from the previous one, as Warden.
The stranger may be kindly, but his purpose is to use the children for his own ends. If
the group do not respond to his offer of help, he may resort to threats. It will be
interesting if he can maintain some kind of secrecy about his occupation, for a time
at least. This is a male role, but there should be no difficulty for female teachers in
taking on this role. If adopting a male role seems to present problems, a female
teacher might become the wife of the Master Sweep.
   Again, it will be important to gauge the interest level of the group. Dramatically,
it may be appropriate for them to reject the Master Sweep's offer, but they may
still be interested in exploring the life of a sweep.

b   One way of introducing the individual activity might be to ask the group for all
the words they can think of which would help to describe the life of a sweep. The
group should work through this activity all at the same time. If some pupils are
working with the kind of quality the teacher is looking for, it may be useful to ask
the rest of the group to watch them for a moment. It will not be external skills

b   *Individual work*
It may be interesting to repeat the circumstances of the escape, whether it has
proved successful or not, as individual movement work. Perhaps each member of
the group continues to remember the escape attempt, and to dream about it.
Music and lighting, if these are available, will assist in creating a dream-like
atmosphere, as will slow-motion movement.

10   CHIMNEY-SWEEPS
This section of the work may be reached in a number of different ways. It could
follow directly from the first section, and be introduced as the charitable lady's
attempt to relieve the children's poverty. Alternatively, the children might have
run away from her, at which point they meet the Master Sweep. If they have
worked through the previous section and their escape has been prevented by the
staff of the workhouse, being apprenticed to the Sweep may be the way in which
the authorities deal with them. If the escape has been successful, and the children
are still together, the next section could follow in this way:

Narrative link
'After their escape from the workhouse, the children travel all night. They have
decided to stay together at first. When daylight comes, they know that a search
might be made for them. Tired and hungry, they take refuge in a derelict
warehouse. . . . As they are resting there, a stranger enters'

a   *Whole group*
The teacher may take on the role of this stranger. He is extremely interested in the
children and where they have come from, but in a very different way to the
charitable person in the first section. He offers the children employment with the
safeguard of a roof over their heads and protection from the workhouse. He points
to himself as an example of a poor boy who is now a solid businessman, and an
employer of others. It should gradually become apparent that he employs
chimney-sweeps.
    The group may accept or reject his offer. If they accept, the work may proceed
as planned. If they reject it, it may still be possible to explore the situation of child
sweeps, but it will need to be introduced in another way. It can be seen as a kind of
'flashback', to what the group have *heard* that the life is like, or to show what *some*
children had to endure in those days.

b   *Individual work*
Each member of the group imagines what it would be like to have to climb a
chimney and sweep it clean of soot. Working non-verbally and individually, each
person goes through the preparations for his day's work, and then lives through a
'day' cleaning chimneys. Slow-motion movement may help here, but what is
required is not necessarily any accuracy of mime, which might present technical

which are commented on, but the way in which the movement reflects thoughts and feelings. The rest of the group might list words suggested by what they have seen in the movement sequence.

   c   Again, this exercise allows reflection on the previous activity.

11   During this questioning, the people involved in the scene should answer in role. Can the onlookers come to any decision about what happened? Who would they blame? How could such accidents be prevented?
   Written work on this section might include:

A newspaper account of the accident.
An official report on the conditions of the climbing children.
A medical report.
An official complaint against the person held to be responsible.

Depending on the ability of the group, the teacher may leave them to handle this discussion by themselves, or she may join in as one of the group or as an adult friend of the children who is interested in what they have been doing.

12   The groups should be discouraged from planning this encounter in too great detail. It will be more interesting if this is an almost spontaneous encounter, so that they discover their reactions and attitudes to the sweep, and do not decide them rigidly in advance. The depth of this piece of work will depend on the ability of the group to maintain the drama for themselves. With an inexperienced group, the scene may become very rambling and inconclusive. They may be engaged in dramatic playing, and the work may be rather superficial. It will be important to discuss what has happened in these scenes, and what the participants have discovered about each other, either before or instead of beginning the next activity.
   A new direction for the drama might arise out of these scenes, and the teacher must be ready to follow any clear leads given by the class. For example, a rich family

problems, but some progression towards a feeling quality associated with such work.

c *In pairs*
The partners describe their day's work to each other. What was the most difficult part of the work? What was the most frightening moment? What did they think about while they worked in the chimneys?

11 THE ACCIDENT

Small groups
Being a chimney-sweep was a dangerous and unpleasant job. Working in small groups, the class show how accidents might have happened. In watching the scenes, the rest of the class will need to consider:

> How did these accidents happen?
> Were they caused by chance or human error?
> Who was responsible?
> What was done to help?

This scene can be either in mime and movement alone, or words may be used. After each scene has been shown, it may be worthwhile to question each person concerned in the scene. This may help to clarify what has happened, but the questions should concentrate not just on the *facts* of what happened, but on the thoughts and feelings of the people involved, and on the consequences of what has happened. Each person might be questioned by two or three others from the rest of the class, or the group as a whole might have to answer questions from the whole class.

12 THE FAMILY IN THE BIG HOUSE

Small groups
Are the climbing children aware of the kind of life which is lived in the large houses whose chimneys they clean? The group may want to consider this question, either in role as the chimney-sweeps, perhaps while they are resting after a hard day's work, or in discussion out of role.

> What have they seen of the life of the house?
> What people from the household have they met?
> What impressions have they formed of the family life?
> What aspects of the life of the household puzzle or confuse them?

Ask the group to imagine that a sweep comes in close contact with the family.

might choose to adopt one of the sweeps. It may be more fruitful to develop an idea like this rather than work through the next activities.

> How will the sweep fit in with their lives?
> What problems may arise?
> What might happen to him in the future?
> How do his old friends react to his good fortune?

13   This kind of short activity can be very useful where the work has not been completed at the end of a lesson, and it is necessary to remind the class of the material they have been working on, and the area of concern. The activity will be particularly useful if the previous scene has been disappointing in its quality.

14   If it seems appropriate, the feedback from the scene of meeting between rich and poor could be handled in discussion, rather than working in pairs and maintaining roles. The choice of activity will depend on the skills of the group.
   Other work might include:

> One of the rich children's diaries, describing the meeting with the sweep.
> A letter of complaint from the master of the house to the Master Sweep.
> A picture of the rich family, or their house.

15   The class will need to be given time to think about this object. It may be helpful to them to discuss the different kinds of rooms there would be in such a house, and

Working in small groups, they should come to some decisions about the family, and choose the moment at which they meet the chimney-sweep. Once they have decided on the opening moment of their scene, it will be valuable if they can develop the rest of the scene by themselves. Some of them will be required to change role and become members of the family or servants, but each group should have at least one sweep in it. The attitudes of the family will be important.

> Is the sweep made welcome or rejected?
> Who is most sympathetic to him?
> What is his response to offers of charity?
> Can he help these people to understand what his life is like?
> What is his reaction to the kind of life by which he is now surrounded?

It may not be appropriate for these scenes to be shown, since they are unrehearsed, but some groups may wish to share one or two moments from their scene – perhaps the beginning or the end of the encounter, or a moment which really revealed the gulf between the sweep and the rich family.

13   RICH AND POOR

Small groups
Ask each group to present a tableau to the rest of the class to show the difference between rich and poor in Victorian society. They can base the tableau on the previous activity, or they can draw on any part of the previous work.

14   SUMMARIZING THE DIFFERENCES

In pairs or threes
Keeping the roles they have developed in the encounter with the family, each person gets together with someone from another group, so that there are two sweeps, two rich children or two parents, or two servants from the household. They discuss with their partners some of the things which happened in their respective scenes.

> What have they learned about the way in which other people live?
> What most surprised them about what they learned?
> Have their attitudes changed in any way?
> Will their behaviour change in future?

15   TEMPTATION

Narrative link
'While the sweeps are working in one of the big houses, they notice something which seems very precious to them. It means so much to them, that they are

the furniture and objects the rooms might contain. What kinds of objects would seem precious to a poor child?

a   Again, if the group find it difficult to maintain the make-believe by themselves, the objects could be described to the group as a whole.

b   It could be that the sweeps are not stealing for their own benefit, but are being used by a gang of criminals to break into the home. If this seems an interesting approach, there may be no need for them to choose an object to steal. Instead, it may be possible to introduce this section by either (1) working in pairs – one is a thief and tries to persuade the other to help him in his theft; (2) in small groups – a gang of thieves force the chimney-sweep to help them.

16   The teacher acts as stage-manager during these scenes. Music and lighting may help to create the atmosphere of the dark and sleeping house. Encourage the groups to think about the climax of their scenes. Is this likely to be the discovery of the crime, or the arrest of the sweep?

17*a,b* and *c*   What is important during this sequence is not necessarily correctness of legal procedure, but the fact that the group is working seriously and with integrity. Considerable formality and seriousness will be required. Defence and prosecution lawyers may need time to prepare their case and talk to their witnesses. If there are insufficient numbers for a full jury of twelve, who will in any case be playing a rather passive role, it may be wiser to make this a magistrate's court with a number of magistrates on the bench.

This section may take a considerable amount of time to work through, and should not be hurried if it seems to be a fruitful experience for the group.

Other work on this section might include:

tempted to steal it the next time they go to the house. The object may be something of great financial value, or it may be something which has great significance for the chimney-sweep, although no one else may value it.'

Ask the group to think about the following questions:

> What is it about the object which tempted them?
> What will they risk if they decide to steal it?
> How will they go about the theft?
> What will they gain from it?

a   *In pairs*
Each sweep describes to his partner the object he wishes to steal. Can he explain what its significance is for him and why he is prepared to take the risk of stealing it?

b   *Individual work*
In movement only, each person works through the circumstances of the theft. It may be appropriate to share some moments from these incidents with the rest of the group.

16   CAPTURE

Small groups
Working in small groups, the class prepare and show a scene in which one of the sweeps is captured during the attempted theft. Words may be used, or the groups may work towards an exaggerated, nightmarish quality by using only movement and sounds. A slow-motion chase or fight sequence might be used, and reactions will need to be very exaggerated to be effective.

17   ON TRIAL

a   *Whole group*
One or more of the sweeps who have been caught stealing are brought to trial. The rest of the class will need to change roles and become judges, advocates, lawyers, witnesses and the jury.

> What is the charge against the prisoner?
> What evidence is there against him?
> What kind of witnesses will be called by the prosecution and the defence?
> Will the prisoner be allowed to speak for himself?
> Are there any extenuating circumstances?
> How will he be sentenced?

This section of the work may make great demands on the abilities of the pupils,

> Written accounts by witnesses of what they had seen or heard.
> A plan of the house, showing how the theft occurred.
> A picture of the object which was stolen.
> A newspaper account of the trial.
> A confession by the thief.

18*a*   This is another point in the work at which the teacher must try to gauge the interest and needs of the group very carefully. What have they learnt so far from the work? Has their understanding of the conditions in Victorian times been increased? Have they been more interested in the plot than in the meanings which might develop from the work? Is it important for them to understand how change comes about? Will they learn more from presenting a case for reform, or from understanding the difficulties of administering charity? What links can the teacher make between this work on Victorian England and problems in the present day?

b   This section of the work will involve the children in research. If the teacher chooses to proceed with this section, she must make sure that the pupils have access to material which will help them in preparing their case.

19   These scenes may include words or may be presented in mime and movement. The information provided can be listed as evidence.

but should also be rewarding. Some of them will be required to change role again, and to preserve a formality of speech and behaviour. It may be helpful to the organization of the activity if the teacher decides to be the Clerk of the Court, who can instruct the other members of the court in the correct procedure, and model appropriate language and behaviour for them.

b *Small groups*
If the prisoner is found guilty, each group may decide what his sentence is to be. They may then tell the rest of the class what happened to him in his later life, or may prepare and show a scene which will give the same kind of information. If the prisoner has been set free, the story of his subsequent career might be told. Did he make good? Was he tempted to commit other crimes?

c *In pairs*
The sweep who was on trial is now twenty years older. He looks back on his life since the trial and describes it to a friend. Is he now a respected member of society, or a hardened criminal? Has he been transported, or is he still in prison?

[Depending on the direction which the drama has taken previously it may be useful to tackle one of the following sections.]

18 REFORM

Whole group
The teacher, in role as chairman of a committee dedicated to the reform of the laws governing children's working conditions, welcomes the class as members of that committee. Their task is to persuade Parliament that the laws need to be changed. They must marshal as much evidence as possible before they present their case. What do they know about working conditions for children at this time? Where did they get their information from? Is it reliable? Since they cannot hope to change things overnight, what are their priorities?

b *In pairs*
One person is a member of the committee for reform. The other is one of the working children. What information can the child provide about daily life and work? How will the reformer use this information?

19 THE EVILS OF CHILD LABOUR

Small groups
Each group prepares and shows a scene which will reveal some of the worst effects of the present laws, perhaps early morning in a miner's family, children crippled by overwork and ill-treatment, or an accident in a factory. These scenes will provide evidence for the work of the reform committee.

20   The role which the teacher chooses will depend on the skills of the group. In role as an MP the teacher can challenge the evidence put forward by the reformers, and help the others to maintain 'Victorian' attitudes. This may be a harder task for the pupils than presenting the case for reform. On the other hand, as one of the reformers, the teacher can help the class in the organization of the case. A third possibility is a neutral, organizing role, in which the teacher may be able to organize the proceedings, and elaborate on points which have been raised by reading depositions which have been received – perhaps statements by powerful factory-owners, or further evidence of the need for reform. (If the teacher is female, as in this case, the obvious points can be made about the licence of taking on the role of an MP in Victorian times!)

21   Although these scenes may be comic in their effect, they are likely to give rise to useful discussion, either in or out of role. It may be possible to contrast Victorian and present-day ideals.

22   This part of the work may help the group to avoid easy solutions to problems. What are the difficulties in administering charity? Should charity be administered privately or is it the duty of the central government? What parallels exist today? What problems have faced international charities? Is there any way to overcome these problems? In what kind of society would charities be unnecessary?

   a   If the teacher is working in role as chairman the narrative link is unnecessary, as the teacher can provide the meeting with this information in role.

20 PRESENTING THE CASE

Whole group
Some members of the class may choose at this point to become the MPs or leaders
of society who have to be convinced of the need for reform. The teacher may join
them or help the rest of the class to present the case for reform. Speakers should
be chosen from the class to present the case. Others may be witnesses, perhaps
from the previous scenes, and these may be cross-examined by both sides.

> How convincing is the case for reform?
> What arguments do the MPs use against it?
> What kinds of evidence will they accept?
> What are the first steps which need to be taken?
> Will reform be a mixed blessing?
> What impact will reform have on the working families?

21 AN IDEAL WORLD

Small groups
Each group shows a brief scene which is of an idealized world. Workers are
cheerful and productive, masters are kind, families are happy, children are
industrious and well cared for. Although these scenes may be exaggerated, they
will give some idea of what the reformers are hoping for.

> How realistic is it to hope that such things might come true?
> What would prevent them coming true?
> How far do these pictures of life conform to a Victorian ideal rather than a
>   modern one?
> Does our life today conform to any of the ideals shown in these scenes?

22 THE CHARITABLE COMMISSION

For this section, the group may keep the roles as reformers which they developed
in the previous section.

Narrative link
'A group of charitable people who are interested in improving conditions for the
poor have been given a certain amount of money by an anonymous donor. They
are to administer this money so that the sufferings of poor children may be
relieved.'

a *Whole group*
The teacher may chair this meeting in role, perhaps as a similar kind of person to
the charitable lady in the first section of the work.

b How sensitive must the charitable person be in approaching the poor person? What are their attitudes to each other?

c At this point in the work, it should be possible for the group to use their experiences from earlier in the drama in order to understand the needs of the poor people. Will this understanding help them to administer charity wisely? Are sympathy and good intentions enough? It will assist the class to think more deeply if the teacher uses the role of chairman to challenge superficial solutions and to strengthen appropriate attitudes.

23   How far does this statue represent some of the things which the class has discovered from the work as a whole?
   Other work might include:

> The rules of the charitable institution.
> Part of the memoirs of one of the charity commissioners.
> The inscription on the base of the statue.

What will the priorities be?
Should the commission concentrate on short-term relief – food and clothing – or should they aim to provide shelter, education and employment?
How will they identify the most deserving cases?
What is the best way to make use of their limited resources?
Is there any way they can increase these resources?

b   *In pairs*
One is a poor person in need of help; the other is one of the charity commissioners. How will the commissioner approach the poor person? Will it be easy to persuade him to accept charity? Will the charity commissioner's priorities be the same as the poor person's? What are the difficulties in this encounter?

c   *Whole group*
The commission comes together again to reach a decision about how the money is to be spent. All the ideas must be clearly presented and if possible a group decision should be reached. Voting may be necessary. This activity may involve a considerable amount of planning. For example, if it is decided to found a hostel or school for homeless children, how will it be set up? What premises will be suitable? What will the rules of the institution be? Will it be possible to administer such a place without its becoming like a workhouse?

After a decision has been reached, it will be important to consider the following questions:

Have the commission decided wisely?
What difference will their charity make?
Will it really affect the lives of poor people as a whole, or just a lucky few?
How will the people who relieve the charity feel about it?

23   THE STATUE

Small groups
Members of the charitable commission, who were highly regarded for their attempts to relieve the sufferings of the poor, are to have a statue erected to their memory. Each small group of three or four pupils creates the statue which would show something of what that person was like, and what they achieved. Each group shows their 'statue' to the rest of the class.

Is this a realistic representation of what this person achieved?
Does it show their attitude to the poor?
What should the inscription on the statue be?

Part 3   *Teaching Drama*

Introduction

This section contains a series of practical notes and checklists. These are designed to assist teachers in defining their aims for a particular lesson, organizing the lesson structure, responding to developments within the drama and evaluating the work. We hope that these practical considerations will assist teachers in setting up and maintaining their own lesson structures and in reflecting purposefully on their efforts.

Planning

Since drama depends for its development on the contributions of the class, there may be difficulties in planning work very far in advance. A tightly-structured lesson may prevent pupils from exploring the material in ways they find relevant. The teacher who sticks doggedly to a lesson plan denies pupils any responsibility for shaping the experience.

Yet while teachers may recognize the importance of building on their pupils' contributions, they may be daunted by the implications of this way of working. Drama requires teachers to be able to think on their feet, and the best way of acquiring this ability is through constant practice based on a clear understanding of the principles of drama and its potential as an educational medium. If teachers lack experience it may be wise for them to go into their lessons with a number of strategies and alternatives carefully planned in advance, but with a readiness to abandon their plans and follow more fruitful directions which seem to engage the interest of their pupils. Growing confidence and expertise will encourage a more flexible approach.

There may be times when it is impossible for teachers to allow any autonomy to their pupils. Some groups cannot function without the teacher's constant support and intervention, either because they lack the social skills to accept the responsibility of working as members of a group, or because they lack the drama skills for operating within the process. With such classes, the teacher may have to start each lesson with a carefully planned progression of tasks designed to encourage the pupils' gradual participation. It may damage the pupils' sense of security if they are presented too quickly with the need for responsible involvement implied in the kind of process we have described, although the achievement of this kind of involvement and responsibility will be a worthwhile educational aim for such classes.

The kind of balance in the work which allows the teacher to operate as a structural agent in the drama and still leaves room for the pupils to influence the development of the work will not be achieved immediately. Instead of working out each phase of the lesson in minute detail, we would encourage teachers to consider the following series of questions as guidelines in planning and carrying out the lesson.

AIMS

What are my aims for this particular lesson?
How do these relate to my long-term aims and objectives for the class?
What kinds of learning can I realistically hope to promote for my pupils, in terms of the issues and implications arising from the drama and in terms of their competence in operating the drama form?

APPROACHES

What is the best way to approach the content of the lesson?
What issues are involved?
Which of these will I select as the initial focus for the drama?
How can I translate this into practical activity – as pair work, small-group scenes, teacher-directed role-play, whole-group 'living through' drama?
Which of these ways of working will be appropriate to the needs of the class and will help them to identify with the situation?
What function will I perform within the drama – instructor, commentator, adviser, chairman, initiator of the drama in role?
How can I make my negotiations as economical as possible?
How much do I need to explain in advance, and why?

DEFINING BOUNDARIES

What controls will I need to provide for this group – limiting the working-space, defining the rules, taking the major share of the responsibility, setting small and clearly defined tasks, restricting physical activity?
What satisfactions is each task likely to provide?

Will the task gain the pupils' commitment?
Are the demands sufficient to challenge them but not to over-tax their social and dramatic skills?
What risks will the pupils be asked to take?
What safeguards can I build into the work in order to help them cope with these?
What are the areas of risk for me?
If there are some risks I am not prepared to take, do I therefore need to alter my plans accordingly?
What are my levels of tolerance in terms of noise, physical activity, sharing responsibility, working spontaneously, the proximity of colleagues, interruption?
Will this class need a gradual introduction to the drama, or should they engage in practical work immediately?
Should the room be rearranged to establish an appropriate atmosphere for the context of the drama?
Should the lesson start in an accustomed way, or are there advantages to be gained from starting in a different style, or with the space arranged differently?

RESPONDING TO DEVELOPMENTS

What adjustments must I make to my original plans if the lesson does not proceed as I had envisaged?
What fresh strategies can I introduce in order to focus the activity?
What kinds of questions will help to direct the pupils' thinking and deepen their commitment?
What fresh challenges should the pupils be faced with?
Will I need to alter or reduce the demands I am making on the pupils?
What unforeseen learning areas are being opened up?
Am I prepared to abandon the learning areas I hoped to achieve and pursue different ones?
What kinds of dramatic structure will help pupils to explore these new areas?
Are my original aims still relevant?
What strategies can I use in order to preserve enough energy to cope with the pressures of teaching drama to a succession of classes, for example, setting a written task?
Will it be appropriate to set such a task to *this* group?
How will I help the class to reflect upon their work?
Will it be appropriate to encourage reflection through discussion or through other modes of expression?
What kinds of question will help me assess what the pupils see as significant in the work?
How will I assess the learning which may have taken place?

Using Theatre Elements

It is not an easy task for teachers to set up drama which actively engages pupils at both an intellectual and an emotional level. As we have pointed out, it should be possible to plan in advance some of the strategies which will be used to engage and sustain the interest of pupils in the drama. One of the most powerful elements in drama is the kind of unpredictability which promotes a spontaneous, authentic response to events. If teachers wish to allow for this element of unpredictability they will not be able to rely on a rigid lesson formula.

It is possible for teachers to achieve a balance which includes some predetermined strategies but which still allows the possibility of creating effective drama in process. To achieve this balance it will be necessary for teachers to employ those elements of dramatic form which are used by playwright, director and actors to create theatre. In theatre, the intention is to promote an experience which engages the attention of the audience on both a thinking and feeling level. In the classroom, teachers will employ similar tools, though under vastly different conditions, in order to set up experiences for the children as participants in the drama.

In this task teachers must be able to:

1   Provide a precise *focus* for the action, one which will pinpoint the problem, topic or issue in a concrete way by indicating:

— the kind of roles or attitudes which the pupils will be asked to represent
— the particular situation in which they are placed
— the task which will initiate the drama.

For example, at a meeting in the village hall, some of the inhabitants of a Mid-Western town are offered free land in Oregon and are asked to decide whether or not they will accept the offer. (Structure 1)

At each successive phase of the work teachers will need to redefine the focus, perhaps by asking themselves, 'What is this work about *now*? How can I create that concern dramatically so that it engages the pupils' interests and yet allows me to fulfil certain objectives in terms of their learning?'

2   Identify and build on the *tensions* inherent in the situation. Sometimes the tension may be set up quite crudely as a direct confrontation and so provide an effective way of releasing or using the energy of a class.
For example, parents oppose their daughter's plans to join the suffragettes. (Structure 10)

At other times it may appear as a dilemma, a threat, a pressure posed by an outside agency or by time factors which demand some kind of response in the very near future.
For example, will the explorers return the baby to the tribe which they have been observing in secret over the past weeks? Does this mean that they will need to reveal their presence and jeopardize the success of the experiment? (Structure 3)

The tensions may not always be fully apparent in the early stages of the work, but may emerge more clearly only as the drama develops and the issues at stake acquire some significance for the participants. Teachers will need to rely on their ability to recognize the tensions implicit in the material and set up appropriate dramatic situations which invite pupils to face the challenges they present.

In order to increase the tension, an element of suspense can be engineered by the teacher working slowly and deliberately in role.

For example, the doctor withholds the little girl's drawings from his colleagues while at the same time building up their expectations as to what they reveal. (Structure 5)

3 Create effective moments of *surprise*, which are dramatic because of their unpredictability. They can lead to a sudden heightening of the tension or introduce an air of watchfulness and apprehension.

For example, the Alien refuses to accept that a male can be captain of the starship. (Structure 13)

4 Use the device of *contrast* to vary the pace of the drama, build a sense of atmosphere and occasion and add to the tension.

For example, the runaways' scramble to avoid detection is followed by a period when they remain quietly on guard. (Structure 4)

5 Employ objects which can help to build belief in the situation and which, with appropriate action, may also come to symbolize meanings beyond the particular context of the drama. Since we cannot predict outcomes in the structures we have described, it is difficult to provide examples of symbols working at the most powerful and effective level, but on occasion objects do acquire some symbolic significance.

For example, after his death, the leader's stick is raised by his followers as a standard to rally all those who will carry on the fight in his name. (Structure 12)

Working in Role

When teachers work in role with a class they are in a position which allows them to structure the drama from *within* the fictional context. By adopting a role appropriate to the situation it is possible to set up and develop drama experiences for the whole class working together as one group. Through the agency of the role teachers can:

Move the pupils into the drama quickly and economically by inviting an immediate response to the intervention of the role.

Provide a model for the pupils' contributions by demonstrating appropriate language, attitudes, actions and commitment.

Present the kind of challenge which may help to focus the pupils' thinking and lead them into a more concerned involvement with the context of the enquiry.

Introduce, in process, those elements of tension, contrast and surprise which can give the experience a heightened dramatic effectiveness, and thereby provide pupils with a model for their own efforts.

Exploit actions and objects so as to lend dramatic significance to their use.

Preserve the continuity of the experience from within.

Offer encouragement and support through their own involvement.

Teaching in role can serve as an excellent strategy for initiating whole-group activities where pupils work through a situation without planning the outcomes in advance. The role presents challenges which cannot be evaded, although pupils may at first take steps to do so. The drama is made out of their thoughts, feelings and actions offered in direct and spontaneous response to these challenges. The particular force of this teaching strategy lies in the qualities of immediacy and spontaneity which it can generate.

Teachers who have not previously worked in this way may experience some initial difficulties. Their pupils may become embarrassed by their involvement in role and greet first attempts with giggles of disbelief. It may be useful to tell them in advance what you intend to do, and even the kind of role you are going to adopt. Often, this need not be very different from a usual teaching role, for example, as the chairman of a meeting. Some children may not find it easy to function as members of a large group or to face the challenges which the role presents. It may take time and perseverance before they begin to meet the demands which are posed.

There may also be a temptation for teachers to use a role as an opportunity for some form of impressive acting display. Though they will need to function as demonstrators and utilize a range of language skills, gestures and attitudes, they must also remain totally aware of the responsibility for structuring an experience for the pupils. The role is simply a device to enter into the make-believe, and everything that the role says and does is dictated by the teacher's concerns as structural agent for the pupils' drama.

When using role, a teacher should ask:

What questions can I ask, *through the role*, which will help to provide a clear focus and slow down the drama?

What challenges can I confront the participants with *in the person of the role*?

What actions can I employ *through the agency of the role* to introduce elements of surprise, contrast or tension?

The teacher never functions as just another participant. If this happens, there is a danger of acting out a separate drama while the pupils pursue or abandon theirs. Repeated practice will give a greater command of the skills necessary for operating in this way.

When working in role it may be helpful to bear in mind some of the following considerations:

What kind of role will be appropriate to the drama? Should it be
— one which carries the authority to command? For example, captain, gang boss, leader.
— one which adopts a humble position? For example, apprentice, new arrival. (Can the teacher cope with this kind of role and hand over a great deal of responsibility to the class? Can the class cope with it?)
— one that takes up a stance that is somewhere between these opposite poles? For example, a go-between, a second-in-command without absolute authority.

What sort of interaction is the role required to promote? Is the purpose to unite the class in energetic opposition to a belligerent autocrat, or to invite their care and concern in dealing with a problem which cannot be coped with alone? For example, a mother comes to ask for help in tracing her lost child.
What kind of language, attitudes and gestures must be selected which will lend conviction to the selected role and promote appropriate responses?
Are the tasks which are asked of the pupils through the role consistent with what that role can legitimately demand? For example, the leader can command that certain things can be done, the new recruit cannot.
What measures can be taken to remove the role from the drama once it is under way, while still allowing for intervention at a later stage? For example, the boss may be called away to meet an important contact, leaving the gang to plan the details of the raid before his return.
What aids are needed which might help to establish the pupils' belief in the role in the drama? For example, a bunch of keys, a file of top-secret documents, the photograph of a missing child.
What steps should be taken to ensure that the pupils know when the teacher is in or out of the drama, or adopting a different role if the situation calls for it?

There are occasions when it is obviously not appropriate to work in role. The setting up of small-group work, for example, is much more quickly achieved by direct instruction, advice and guidance, with the teacher out of role, since this particular mode provides for a different form of experiencing. When problems arise in the course of whole-group drama which the role cannot legitimately handle, then this is more effectively dealt with by stopping the drama and sorting out the difficulties in discussion. Though discipline problems can often be coped with by the teacher in role without affecting the development of the work, it may ultimately be necessary to stop the drama and point out the destructive effects of such behaviour. There is little point in persisting with the role if the make-believe context has ceased to exist for all but the teacher.

Role-taking can provide an effective and economical means of structuring in process. It is a strategy all drama teachers might profitably have at their command for use when, and if, appropriate.

When pupils also adopt roles the challenge of actively identifying with the role is one of the most valuable elements in drama. When working in role, pupils do not merely imitate observed behaviour, but combine many details in an imaginative way. To do this effectively, they must draw on their own knowledge and experience in order to select appropriate behaviour for the role. They learn flexibility, concentration and control. They receive cues from the group and the environment, and learn to discipline their responses in relation to the context. This self-discipline grows from their own understanding and is also a social discipline since they must recognize and adjust to the requirements of the dramatic situation, the dynamics of the group and the developing meaning of the work. Through engaging in active role-play, pupils become increasingly capable of co-operation and social interaction. They learn to observe reality and may acquire new concepts through the drama, as well as building on the experience and knowledge of the others in the group. As different roles in different situations are undertaken, so pupils grow in their capacity to respond appropriately and effectively within the drama.

Questioning

Skilful questioning is likely to be one of the drama teacher's most useful tools. At the beginning of a lesson, questions can be used to establish the context of the drama; during the lesson to involve the participants and to deepen and focus their thinking; and after the lesson, to reflect upon and evaluate the experience.

One of the teacher's traditional roles is that of 'questioner', most often in order to check on the learning of the class. A question will usually elicit a response, but it is the kind of question which is asked which will determine the response which is given. Most teachers' questions are a way of gaining information, of checking facts, of measuring how much detail the pupils may have accumulated, and too often the 'correct' answer already exists in the teacher's mind. There is a single required response which the pupils must produce as quickly as possible. Questioning in drama will have a very different purpose from this kind of questioning. In drama, there is no right answer. The teacher is not asking questions to which there is a single appropriate response.

The least useful kinds of questions in drama will be those which merely check facts, evoke obvious answers or lead to 'yes/no' responses. These basic responses may be accepted by the teacher if the pupil is hesitant, unsure or unused to this way of working. A 'yes' or 'no' answer may at the very least indicate that the group are prepared to accept and go along with what is happening, although they are not yet ready to offer more personal or positive contributions. These kinds of answer may also mean that they are waiting to see what develops – to make sure that they understand the context before they risk making an individual contribution. They may be learning through these limited answers just what is appropriate – what are the rules of the game. Later, as pupils realize that it is on their responses that the drama is built, the teacher can challenge them more directly through questioning.

The drama teacher can use questions to establish atmosphere, feed in information, seek out the interests of the group, determine the direction of the drama, give status to the participants, challenge superficial thinking, control the class, draw the group together to confront specific problems, and guide reflection on the work. The responses of the class will demonstrate a great deal about the level of their thinking.

Useful kinds of questions are:

Questions which set the scene:
What are you children doing hiding in my barn? (Structure 4)
How long have we been in this desert? (Structure 1)
Information-seeking questions:
Can you remember the day we left our homes? (Structure 11)
Where do the people of the tribe meet? (Structure 3)
How shall we prepare for our night in the haunted house? (Structure 7)
Questions to locate the group in space and time:
Base control to Starship – are you receiving me? (Structure 13)
Is this the room in which the ghost was seen? (Structure 7)
Questions to stimulate research:
What would a chimney-sweep earn in Victorian times? (Structure 4)
How many days will it take us to reach America? (Structure 11)
Questions that contain information:
How many guards do we need to defend Hrothgar's hall? (Structure 12)
Are your weapons ready for inspection? (Structure 12)
Questions that give control:
How can we move so that the Indians won't hear us? (Structure 1)
Are you ready to sign up for this expedition? (Structure 3)
How can we set up this courtroom so that justice is done? (Structure 8)

In the pressure to ask open-ended questions, teachers should avoid falling into the trap of being so open that the class are unable to understand or respond. Equally, they must be sure that they can cope with the answers to the questions they have asked.

Discussion and Reflection

An essential element in drama teaching is the ability to make effective use of classroom discussion. This is likely to require as much skill as the structuring of the drama itself, and will make considerable demands on the judgement and sensitivity of the teacher. But because discussion is clearly seen to be so important there is a danger that it may be over-used. It can happen that the drama activity diminishes until it has become merely a stimulus to or a starting-point for discussion, which is regarded as the real core of the lesson. There are lessons where a well-handled discussion can draw learning from what may have been a superficial drama experience, and lessons where a brief drama activity may lead to a most valuable discussion, but it would be unwise to rely on discussion to salvage ineffectual drama. It is important that active discovery and learning remain an essential part of the experience, and that the teacher does not come to depend on discussion to justify the work.

Discussion will be particularly useful and appropriate when the teacher is:

> Preparing for a new piece of work.
> Finding ways into fresh material.
> Considering alternative points of view.
> Reviewing the progress of the drama.
> Deciding on a course of action or a new direction for the work.
> Defining and resolving problems posed by the context or the form.
> Evaluating achievement.
> Reflecting on the work.

Discussion for these various purposes is likely to take place outside the drama. It is wise to keep initial discussion of work to an appropriate minimum. Some teachers feel that extensive discussion is necessary before the drama can begin, and this kind of introductory session may be important for some groups. For others, a lengthy discussion may dissipate enthusiasm and lead to frustration. Another difficulty is that an interesting discussion may raise so many issues that the teacher cannot find a clear focus for the start of the drama. It may be more effective to capitalize on initial interest and curiosity and begin the drama almost immediately. Some of the introductory activities in these structures give the opportunity for discussion and the sharing of existing knowledge and information within the drama. For example, the poor children describing their situation to the philanthropic lady, the discussion about whether to accept the offer of £50 for spending a night in the haunted house, or the detectives examining evidence.

The function and shape of such activities may be very much that of a discussion, but the pupils and the teacher are already in role, even if only vestigially, and this will help to focus the talk. The class will also feel that the drama has begun, and will recognize that they have a share in building it. As soon as the teacher feels it to be necessary, the drama activity can be interrupted for further clarification in discussion out of role.

The quality of the discussion is likely to be improved if teachers can:

> Give a clear focus to the talk.
> Seek clarification of ideas.
> Encourage pupils to ask their own questions and give them time to formulate answers.

> Make their own contributions clear and to the point.
> Summarize various points of view and their implications for action.

The most frequent use of class discussion is likely to be in reflecting on the drama experience. Gavin Bolton has said that 'experience in itself is neither productive nor unproductive; it is how you reflect on it that makes it significant.' But reflection need not take the form of discussion immediately after the drama. Indeed, this may be the least appropriate time. Discussion may blur and dissipate what has been a significant experience, and the teacher may fail to recognize what the experience has actually been for the pupils. Reflection need not necessarily take the form of discussion, nor need it occur when the experience is complete. It is possible to include reflection as part of the dramatic context, so that participants can discover what the experience means to them during the course of the drama.

Reflection within the drama is likely to be more powerful than end-of-session discussion, since it allows individual and group insight to be articulated as part of the context. This kind of reflection might include:

> The starship's flight log. (Structure 13)
> The emigrant's diary. (Structure 11)
> The report to the Reform Committee on conditions in the workhouse. (Structure 4)
> The treaty drawn up with the Indians. (Structure 1)
> The settlers' map. (Structure 1)
> The statements of witnesses to the robbery. (Structure 8)
> The ritual before the hunt. (Structure 3)
> The dance of celebration. (Structure 1)
> The TV programme at the end of the experiment. (Structure 3)

A useful strategy for encouraging reflection in an action-oriented class is to introduce a role, perhaps that of visitor, commentator or outsider. For example, a reformer visiting the workhouse, a scientist examining the progress of the experiment, a journalist, a superior checking on progress. These roles are designed solely to engage the pupils in reflective talk about their activities, environment or situation. Activities which move the participants backwards or forwards in time can prove effective in encouraging reflection – the emigrants' dream of the future, the settlers' memory of the life they have left behind.

All of these are forms of reflection which can be set up as part of the drama and which will enrich the experience. Some will require that the drama experience is transferred into another expressive mode, and one which may not require a verbal response. The pupils' involvement in such tasks may provide further material for use in the drama, or may even act as a powerful focus for what follows – the map which is stolen or destroyed by enemies, the letter from the workhouse inmate which the governor refuses to deliver, the treaty which is torn up. Such tasks may also, at a simple level, allow the teacher time to consider the development of the work, and provide time for forward planning.

Evaluation and Assessment

In evaluating drama, it is the quality of the experience which is important. Drama experience which has been worthwhile educationally will arouse curiosity, strengthen initiative, offer pupils opportunities for using their wits, resources and skills in unpredictable situations, increase their sense of what is appropriate, demonstrate how responsibility operates, both personally and within the group and help them to understand how people change and develop in response to their circumstances. The kind of growth in understanding which a worthwhile drama experience can promote will be a step towards maturity for the participants.

Every significant experience takes up something from what has gone before and lives on in further experience, modifying in some way those experiences which follow it. This kind of continuity and interaction, as well as the adaptation which must ensue if the activity is to be really educational, provides the educative value and significance of the drama experience.

Among the problems which may arise in attempting to assess the quality of the drama experience will be the group nature of the work and the fact that one has to be guided by externals in judging what may be largely an inner experience. But of necessity, teachers must constantly try to assess their own work and that of their pupils. Without the feedback provided by effective assessment it will be difficult for either teachers or pupils to make progress. Consciously or unconsciously, at every stage of the lesson, the teacher will be judging the group's level of interest in the theme, the effectiveness of the strategies which are being used, and the engagement of the pupils with the developing meaning of the work.

In assessing the drama experience, teachers may wish to begin by examining their own contribution to the work. It may be useful to look at the teacher's contribution to the lesson in terms of the suggestions in the chapters on 'The Drama teacher' and 'Planning'. The teacher's objectives for a particular class must be realistic, and effective strategies must be selected in order to achieve these objectives. If the structures suggested in this book have been used, were they appropriate to the needs of the class and the aims of the teacher? Is there any danger that particular strategies will become stale and familiar through over-use? Does the teacher remain flexible in response to the changing needs of the class and the demands of the material?

The engagement of the pupils in the meaning which is being created and the growth in insight and understanding can be judged partly by externals. The atmosphere in the room, the level of commitment to the work, the ways in which pupils reflect on the experience, both within the drama and outside it, their capacity to see wider implications and to draw parallels between the dramatic situation and the real world, and their transformation of the drama experience into other expressive modes, will all be measures of the significance of the experience.

PROGRESS IN DRAMA

The kind of progress in drama which a pupil is likely to make over a period of time will not just be to do with an increased technical competence in using the drama medium. Teachers should ask whether there is an increase in the level of complexity in what is being created in the drama – the feelings, ideas, events and relationships which are being explored and represented. The ability to describe, analyse, interpret and evaluate are all important in aesthetic experience and if there is progress in drama one would expect an increase in competence in these abilities. An increased skill in working with drama and theatre forms is to be expected, as is the ability to use the elements of theatre in order to negotiate and develop meaning. There may be an enhanced capacity in performance, in encapsulating a shared drama experience and communicating it to others by turning it into theatre.

The qualities and skills which might be expected to develop from several years' work in drama might include the following:

A willingness to co-operate with the rest of the group.
An awareness of and sensitivity to what is being created in the drama.
The ability to adopt, sustain and develop a role.
The ability to initiate ideas for the group.
A willingness to respond to and develop the ideas of others.
An ability to understand and explore the dramatic situation.
The capacity to respond appropriately both verbally and non-verbally within the action.
The willingness to take risks and tackle the unexpected.
Increased confidence and competence in using different forms of drama to create and explore meaning.
The ability of pupils to reflect on and evaluate their own work.

Some practical considerations

Since drama requires the active involvement of the participants, it is essentially an exploratory process which needs both time and a sense of continuity. Neither of these needs is well served by single lessons of thirty-five or forty minutes. The pressures of time can prove inimical to the slow and careful negotiations required in drama.

The group nature of the work may force pupils to make major adjustments to their attitudes when they come to the drama lesson. For most of their time in secondary school, pupils may be asked to function in situations where the emphasis is on individual effort and achievement. It is not surprising that many pupils may find it difficult to accept the responsibilities of group collaboration. The apparent freedoms offered both by the nature of the activity and by the teacher's stance as co-author and not chief instructor may present problems.

In many schools the space available for drama fails to provide the kind of privacy or atmosphere which will foster concentrated attention on the task in hand, although teachers may be more aware of interruptions than their pupils. Suitable resources may also be lacking.

Some of these difficulties can be overcome or minimized. We hope that the notes accompanying the structures will indicate practical suggestions, but it may also be helpful for teachers to consider the following points.

TIME

Where classes are time-tabled for single periods, it may be wise for teachers to move into the drama as quickly as possible. Excessive time spent in such activities as registration, changing into special clothing etc., may take up so much of the lesson that the pupils cannot become actively involved in the drama itself and are denied any sense of achievement and satisfaction. It is better to spend the time *doing* drama rather than preparing to do it.

The use of various aids can provide valuable short cuts into the subject matter, especially if this has to be reintroduced after a week's gap. Maps, photographs, letters, drawings, diary entries and tape-recordings can be used effectively. These may have been made by the pupils themselves as part of the previous week's work, or have been prepared by the teacher in the interim. Devices such as the use of narrative links or the creation of 'still photographs' or tableaux can be useful in moving the drama quickly from one phase to the next.

There may also be a need for considerable flexibility in the way that teachers allocate their time during the lesson.

For instance, it may take longer than anticipated for pupils to prepare work for showing. If they are productively engaged in this task, it would be sensible to extend the original time limit, provided that each contribution can still be accommodated in the time left available. There is sometimes a tendency for teachers to move rapidly from one task to the next. It may be more valuable to stay with an activity which seems to engage the purposeful, serious attention of the pupils and abandon the original lesson plan.

SPACE

Because drama involves an element of physical activity, it is sometimes considered impossible to attempt it without a large working space. This is not necessarily the case. A vast, echoing hall can hinder the development of quiet, thoughtful enquiry. Teachers may have to spend time in creating appropriate conditions out of an apparently unsuitable environment, but it is possible to reorganize an ordinary desk-filled classroom to provide an adequate working area. The furniture can perhaps be cleared to one side, the task being incorporated into the routine at the start of the lesson. A circle of chairs within that area will usually serve as an adaptable arena for many forms of drama activity.

Conversely, the difficulties of working in a very large space can be reduced by marking off a part of the room with chairs, benches or masking-tape, and confining the work within the defined space.

The kind of activity which is possible will obviously be determined by the actual physical conditions in which the drama takes place. Large-scale movement work will not be appropriate in a small, cluttered area.

What may be more important than the actual size of the room is the way in which the space is used to reinforce the context of the drama. A gang hide-out, a forest clearing, an office, a prison can be effectively suggested with a different arrangement of the furniture and the general layout of the room.

CONTROLS AND GUARANTEES

Many teachers see loss of control as one of their greatest fears in the drama lesson. Because the activity depends on group effort and is given expression through talk and movement, they may doubt their ability to focus and contain the pupils' contributions. They worry that the active participation of the class may degenerate into chaos. This worry will be increased by the proximity of the drama room to other classrooms and offices. There is no easy answer to this problem of location, though teachers' anxieties may be alleviated in part if they can win the support and understanding of colleagues and gain their recognition of the difficulties involved in creating drama.

Some rules may be necessary. What these are depends on individual teachers, their classes, the type of drama they seek to do and their working conditions. These rules may be worked out by teacher and pupils in consultation. They may govern conduct within the drama room. For example, 'The area where the dining tables are stacked is out of bounds because of the danger of overturning them.' They may also relate to the making of the drama itself. For example, 'Everyone agrees to sustain the make-believe and offer contributions which will assist the group's collaboration'.

Teachers may also find it useful to have certain control devices which are clearly recognizable and as clearly obeyed. Of the key words which signal a halt to the activity in progress, 'Freeze' is perhaps the most common example. Moving to or sitting in a particular part of the room can also be a way for teachers to indicate that a break in the activity is called for. The following strategies can also provide a useful measure of control:

Slow-motion movement.
Making tableaux, still photographs, portraits, waxworks, statues.
Using games with clearly-defined rules as part of the make-believe context of the drama, for example, 'Keeper of the Keys' as a test of stealth. (Structure 12)
The teacher working in role within the drama.

> Role-play situations in which only a few pupils are actively involved at any one time and work inside a circle formed by the rest of the class. (Structure 5)
> Changing the activity from drama to another kind of task – writing, drawing, map-making.

There may be occasions when almost an entire lesson is best given over to writing or drawing. The results may be used profitably as preparation for subsequent developments. The need for this kind of activity will be dictated by the demands of the material as well as by the mood of the class. It may be a way of usefully varying the activity at those moments when the drama fails to capture the pupils' interest and the teacher is unable to find an alternative strategy.

In some cases pupils may misbehave because they are asked to participate in activities which they do not find sensible and whose purposes they do not understand. They may also lack sufficient skills to cope with the tasks set by the teacher and may become frustrated, or embarrassed by their failure to deal with these demands, especially when they know that the results of their work are to be shown to the rest of the class. Pupils will often defend themselves against pressure of this kind by making hostile or facetious comments, or by simply refusing to participate. They may be acutely aware that the rewards are simply not great enough to justify the risks involved.

It is possible for the teacher to build certain safeguards into the work which can help to protect pupils against these risks. These safeguards include:

> Establishing an atmosphere of trust and encouraging even the most limited contributions.
> Setting up work which has a clear focus and contains clearly defined tasks which are within the capacity of the class.
> Providing a model of appropriate behaviour and commitment, most effectively perhaps by taking a role within the drama.
> 'Distancing' material which may prove embarrassing to the pupils by setting it within an analogous situation.
> Offering constant reminders that the pupils are working in an art form which will legitimately permit them to explore thoughts and feelings through the safety of an adopted role.

If behaviour problems continue to threaten the development of the work, the teacher may need to resort to the usual disciplinary sanctions and stop the activity. Used positively, the ensuing discussion may provide both teacher and pupils with an excellent opportunity to look at the problems which have arisen and examine possible solutions. Such discussions need not only be concerned with matters of behaviour. The teacher can ask for his or her pupils' opinions on the possible development of the drama and invite their comments on and analysis of the work. After all, drama is a collaborative activity. If pupils are offered opportunities for this kind of sharing they may recognize more readily that they do have a real responsibility for its outcome.

Part 4 *Structures for Development*

Introduction

In this final section, eleven different introductory lessons are described. The approaches outlined in these lessons have proved successful with several classes of varying backgrounds and abilities. We also indicate ways in which drama techniques can be used effectively in other subject areas. In each case the introductory lesson is described in some detail and a number of suggestions are made for the possible development of the work.

We hope that teachers who have absorbed the strategies and teaching-points covered in detail in the earlier structures (1–4) will be able to use these introductory lessons as starting-points for their own work. They should gain confidence and a flexibility of approach from an increased familiarity with the different strategies, techniques and modes of dramatic activity described in the structures.

Drama as enquiry

In one sense all drama is concerned with the process of enquiry, with finding out
why certain people behave as they do in response to a particular set of circumstances. The first three lessons described in this section of the book use this spirit
of enquiry by posing mysteries that need to be solved (Structure 5: *Mystery
Pictures*; Structure 6: *Detectives*; Structure 7: *The Haunted House*). Although the
three lessons are very similar in terms of organization and tasks, each one offers a
different stimulus for the investigation. This kind of approach is easily adapted to
other contexts, for example trying to piece together the mystery of the person who
has lost her memory, or the race of people who have left behind only a few clues
about their history and way of life.

This approach provides a way of beginning the drama very quickly with a
minimum of introductory discussion.

The objects or pictures used as clues provide an effective focus for gaining
and holding the attention of the pupils.

The mystery element is a strong motivating force and the task is clear – there
is a mystery to be solved.

The drama can develop according to the pupils' own interests since they, as
investigators, experts, or anthropologists, are responsible for choosing the
avenues of exploration they wish to follow.

It is usually a straightforward matter for the teacher to set up the appropriate
dramatic situation which will support and promote their investigations.

This approach encourages speculation, interpretation, and the forming of
hypotheses.

Skills of co-operation, and concentration are encouraged and opportunities
exist for decision-making.

Since there are no 'right answers', the pupils may return to the starting-point
and construct alternative versions of the events. The opportunity to examine
the problem from different angles may help to keep the work fresh over
several lessons. The format is equally useful for teachers faced with covering
a single lesson, or with a new class.

Small-group work

Some pupils enjoy working in small groups and preparing scenes which they then present to the other members of the class. They may come to regard drama as consisting solely of this kind of activity and teachers will then have difficulty in persuading them to abandon a familiar format and attempt work of a different kind. Small-group work alone is not the best way for drama to achieve its full potential as a means of learning, but the small-group starters described here show how material was subsequently developed in greater depth. (Structure 8: *Young Offenders*; Structure 9: *Disaster*; Structure 10: *Suffragettes*.) In most of these examples the classes were skilled at handling the complex tasks of selecting, shaping and presenting ideas. Where these skills do not exist, teachers may find it essential to offer advice and guidance so that this mode of dramatic activity is used to provide a strong starting-point for the ensuing work.

Drama across the curriculum

Structures 11 to 15 have been chosen to show how drama strategies can be used to teach specific topics, to illuminate particular areas of the curriculum or to introduce drama approaches to an inexperienced class.

Emigrants (Structure 11) offers another example of the way in which drama can be used to set up an active exploration of historical themes. It invites pupils to identify with a particular group of people and with their predicament, though the teacher may want to use the questions raised to help pupils look at more contemporary parallels. The theme of this lesson is almost identical to that of 'The Way West' and could be developed in a similar way.

Myths and legends often feature in English, integrated studies and humanities courses. When using legends in the drama lesson, teachers sometimes feel that the strength of the narrative actually inhibits them from doing any more than merely re-enacting the story-line.

Beowulf (Structure 12) shows that it is possible to extend the themes rather than simply re-enact plot.

Starship (Structure 13) attempts to show how a specific issue, in this case sexism, can be made dramatically explicit, so that pupils' existing attitudes and responses are challenged.

Macbeth (Structure 14) demonstrates the use of drama strategies to extend pupils' knowledge of an examination text. The strategies described could be applied to most novels, plays and narrative poems which pupils might be required to study in English lessons.

Advertising Campaign (Structure 15) is an appropriate starting-point for approaching drama with an inexperienced and unmotivated class. It should give the class confidence in their ability to work in drama and increase their understanding of one aspect of the media.

TEACHING NOTES

Since the teacher did not know this group he needed a structure which would:

1   Provide him with the security of a pre-planned starting-point.
2   Get the drama started quickly and give the class the satisfaction of engaging with the topic without a lengthy initial discussion.
3   Allow for flexibility of development and the opportunity to change the kind of dramatic activity if whole-group work proved unsuitable.

1*a*   The teacher does not comment on the exact nature of the expertise. This can be decided upon once the drama gets under way and when both he and the pupils have some idea of what could prove relevant. He also wishes to allow for a variety of expert opinion.

The teacher's role signals professionalism and concern. Though he has called this meeting together and is, therefore, officially in charge, he conveys recognition of his colleagues' status in the language he uses to address them. He speaks quietly and with some urgency. As teacher, he feels the need to attract interest and attention as quickly as possible.

Story-telling techniques will be important here in helping to create an air of mystery. For example, variations in pace, making eye-contact with the listeners, building suspense.

The teacher deliberately chooses to make the child this age in order to awaken their concern for someone who is several years younger.

5 Mystery Pictures

This topic was begun with a mixed second-year class, in a classroom for a double period of sixty-five minutes.

The teacher had not worked with this group before. They had asked to do some drama about 'a horror mystery'. His intention was to provide a strong initial focus, but one that would be open-ended enough to allow the pupils to develop their own interests in the theme.

PREPARATION

The teacher needs to prepare two pictures in advance – see *Narrative link* below and 1*b* on following page.

1 THE MYSTERY

a *Whole group*
The teacher explains that he will be asking the class to work as one group. He will take on a role as the head of a special unit in a hospital, and they will need to adopt the roles of experts whose help is needed in dealing with a particular patient whose case is causing him great concern. It presents a mystery which he cannot solve.

The pupils seat themselves in a square representing the doctor's office. He greets them in role and apologizes for breaking into their busy professional schedules. He hopes that the discussion will not take up too much of their valuable time but assures them that their advice and guidance will be of great importance. He reminds them of the confidential nature of the case: nobody is to discuss it outside that room. He then gives them the following details.

Narrative link
'There is a young child in my care at this hospital, who is seven years old. She was brought here several days ago following a mysterious incident at her home. One

b   The pictures must be prepared beforehand. They can be very simply drawn on foolscap paper in felt-tip pen. In this instance, they should show the bedroom walls, a bed, a window, a lamp, some chairs, a dolls' house, three dolls and a few other toys.

Each contribution is made with total seriousness and, though perhaps a third of the pupils do not make a verbal commitment to the drama, the teacher is aware of the high level of interest and absorption.

c   This is done in the same slow, deliberate manner as before. The teacher builds the suspense by delaying the moment when he reveals what this drawing contains. It shows the child's bedroom in a state of confusion: toys are ripped apart, the doll's house destroyed, the windows wide open etc. There is considerable damage.

morning her parents found her sitting outside her bedroom door. When they entered the room they found it to be in a state of some confusion. "It was wrecked," they said. They asked their daughter what had happened but she refused to speak. She has not spoken since. She is obviously very shocked, though she is physically well. The only way in which she has made any reference to what happened during the night has been in the form of two pictures. She drew them yesterday. The first one shows her bedroom in its usual state. The second one shows it in the condition in which her parents found it when they went in there on that morning a few days ago.'

b   *Questions: first picture*

The teacher slowly removes the drawings from the folder he carries with him. He shows the first of these to the group, allowing sufficient time for them to study it carefully. They may ask for certain details to be explained. Wherever possible, the head of the unit provides them with answers, though he tells them that some information is still not available. The group then ask questions about the child, her home and family. For example:

> What is her name?
> Where is her room in relation to the parents' bedroom?
> Which floor is it on?
> Has she always slept in this room?
> Does the picture show all her toys and possessions or only a selection of them?
> Which of the toys are her favourites?
> Who bought those for her?
> Is she a happy child?
> Does she have any brothers and sisters?
> Does she play in this room?
> Has she shown the drawing to her parents?

The head of the unit asks why they find such questions significant. How can enquiries of this kind help to throw light on the mystery? In suitably 'professional' tones these pupils explained that the selection of items in the picture may have some relevance. It may provide a lead which they could follow up.

During this interchange the contributors were asked if they would like to identify their particular expertise. Amongst others, there were specialists in hypnotism, the supernatural, children's illnesses and psychiatry.

c   *Questions: second picture*

The second drawing is shown to the class and placed side by side with the first so that a direct comparison can be made. The head of the unit asks the experts to comment on the differences. He invites their questions and asks if they can begin

The development of this lesson cannot be predicted in advance. In this case the children began to move the direction of the drama away from the kind of 'horror' situation envisaged by the teacher, i.e. one created by supernatural forces. The pupils became more and more concerned with finding out about the child herself and with investigating the reasons for her actions. The teacher had no choice but to respond to the direction in which the enquiry now seemed to be heading. The pupils decided that the child might have been trying to seek some kind of revenge on her parents or that she may have caused the damage in her sleep and is now afraid to talk about the incident.

The teacher was faced with a difficult decision. He was concerned to maintain the level of seriousness which had been shown up to this point. One way for him to do this would have been to switch to the role of the father and make appropriate interventions and challenges through that role. If the teacher handed over this responsibility to one of the pupils he might be putting the drama at risk if the child was unable to maintain the make-believe or offer sensible and serious contributions. The boy chosen proved to be excellent in both respects.

2   The teacher's role allows him to make occasional suggestions and convey signs of approval. He also takes notes and asks for questions and answers to be repeated if he wants them to be given further consideration. (He is a slow note-taker!)

This is a lengthy session but again the attention of the class is held completely. There are very few pupils who have failed to make some contribution by this stage.

The boy now begins to talk as the expert talking about the father! His contributions continue to be very valuable. He draws his colleagues' attention to the significance of certain comments made by the father and helps the teacher to focus

to make tentative suggestions which would help to explain the causes of the mysterious happening. They may want to know such details as:

> Were there any signs of an intruder?
> Did the parents hear any sounds coming from the child's room?
> Was the child in any way destructive?
> How did she get on with her parents?
> Did they ever physically rebuke her?
> Had there been any similar occurrence in the past?

They now begin to construct a possible explanation of events, and in this case wondered whether the destruction might not have been caused by the child herself. They used the pictures as evidence in support of their theory and referred to their experience in other cases of this kind.

The head of the unit says that he is impressed with their expertise. He is grateful for their interpretation of the pictures but remarks that theories will need to be looked at more closely. He asks what the next step might be.

The group members in this case decided that they would like to question some of the people involved in the case. They wanted to meet the father first of all.

The teacher came out of role and asked if there was someone who would be prepared to represent the father. He warned that whoever agreed to do so would have the responsibility for helping the enquiry to proceed with the same quality of seriousness and concentration that had been shown so far. The teacher chose one of several volunteers, asked him to leave his seat at the conference table and wait 'outside the office'.

2 QUESTIONING THE FATHER

Whole group

The father is brought into the meeting. The head of the unit welcomes him, and explains that the people present know some of the details of his daughter's case. They have the kind of knowledge which might help to clear up the mystery and help the little girl to recover from her shocked state.

The father answers the experts' questions. The teacher is able to hand over the conduct of the interview to the class and makes very infrequent comment on what occurs. In this instance, the father responded to each of the queries with total seriousness and proved extremely capable at using details already raised in previous discussion to focus the line of development which was now being pursued. For example, he told the group that the child was very solitary and had few friends, that he was often working away from home, and that there had been a younger sister who had died as a baby.

The head of the unit intervenes to bring the session to a close. He thanks the father for his co-operation. The pupil who has taken this role returns to his seat at the table and joins the rest of the group in a discussion about the information they

the discussion on what the interview has revealed about this parent's attitude. [Although the main activity involved the class in what might appear as little more than an in-role discussion, the first session has been recorded in detail to illustrate the kind of interest and absorption which a starting-point of this nature can sometimes promote. It should be remembered, though, that each group will interpret the material in a different way and that the teacher must be prepared to accept what the class is offering and set up situations which will help them to explore *their* interests.]

3b   The teacher can secretly ask the girl if she wishes to prolong the sense of mystery by remaining silent at this stage of the work.

have gained and about the father's reaction under questioning. These pupils wanted to interview other people connected with the case, namely the mother, the child's teacher and a friend. They thought it would also be useful to see the child herself and try to get her to talk to them.

3   FURTHER DEVELOPMENTS

Other strategies that might be used in subsequent lessons to develop the work include:

> *a*   Interviewing the mother, the child's teacher and a schoolfriend in order to obtain their views of the case. These roles can be taken by other members of the group. The interviews can be conducted by the whole group, or in smaller groups or in pairs who report back to the others.
>
> *b*   Observing the child's reactions to her parents. This can be set up in a room with a 'two-way' mirror, which enables the experts to watch the meeting and comment on the results while remaining unseen. The parents are taken to see the child individually and then together. They talk with her and try to persuade her to speak to them.
>
> *c*   Showing scenes from family life based on the parents' evidence. The pupils suggest situations which might help to show the experts how things had been before the mystery occurred. Groups perform their interpretations and the observers watch (as experts) and comment on the significance of the events witnessed. Certain parts of the scenes may be replayed for greater clarification. What effect did the events have on the child?
>
> *d*   Small-group scenes offering alternative interpretations of how the damage was caused to the child's bedroom. Groups prepare their version of what *might* have happened. For example, the child sleepwalks, there is a supernatural visitation, the dolls themselves become the destroyers etc.
>
> *e*   Role-play activities trying out the ways in which the parents could persuade the little girl to return home when made well. The experts role-play the characters involved under the direction of the head of the unit and test out the most suitable approaches.

TEACHING NOTES

This kind of class can present the drama teacher with a variety of problems. The pupils possessed a high level of energy, which needed to be channelled constructively if the class were to achieve any satisfaction from the work.

Since the class had difficulty in pretending, the teacher chose real objects to hold their interest and focus their attention. It is important that the pupils begin to see the implications of the 'clues', and follow these up in their questioning. In the actual choice of objects it is the possibility of implications which will guide the teacher in making the selection. It may not be necessary to include quite so many 'clues'. The photograph might be of the girl herself, of her family, or of the house.

I   The teacher raises the status of the class by suggesting that they are competent detectives and asking for their help. She is beginning to define their roles as 'experts'.

A balance has to be maintained between providing the group with too little information to interest them and overwhelming them with numerous 'facts'.

The teacher has not invented a story in advance, but creates Anne's background in response to the questions of the group. She is deliberately evasive about a number

6 *Detectives*

This lesson took place with a second-year class in a drama room during a single period.

The class found it difficult to become involved in drama. The pupils lacked concentration, often refused to commit themselves to the make-believe and seldom worked co-operatively. They found role-play embarrassing, and had few drama skills. The teacher was seeking a starting-point which would involve the group in a co-operative enquiry and one which would challenge them without putting too great a pressure on their limited drama skills. A specific objective for this first session was to encourage them to listen, to the teacher and to each other.

PREPARATION

At the beginning of the lesson, the teacher brings a number of objects into the drama room, such as: a necklace; a pill bottle; a large photograph of a teenage girl; an alarm clock. On the blackboard she scrawls the word 'Boathouse — '.

1 THE DISAPPEARANCE

Whole group
The teacher introduces herself as coming from Scotland Yard. She has been given to understand that the pupils are all competent detectives. She needs their help. They have been called in to assist her in solving what is a rather baffling case.

On the previous night, a young girl disappeared from her home. Her name was Anne Robinson and she was 16. She was last seen when the housekeeper said goodnight to her at 10 p.m. When the housekeeper went to Anne's room at 8 a.m. the following morning, she had disappeared. Her bed had not been slept in, and there were some signs of a struggle. The alarm clock had been found on the floor, and had stopped at 11 p.m. Robbery did not appear to have been a factor in her

of aspects of the case, for example, the contents of the pill bottle, since these may provide the basis for future investigations, which the group can carry out.

2   It may prove difficult at this point to get the class to accept each other's ideas. A class which finds it possible to operate in small groups may prefer to develop a group hypothesis, and present it to the rest of the class.

To assist them, the teacher makes a list on the blackboard of all the significant facts which should be taken into consideration in any theory about the girl's disappearance.

If the teacher perceives that the class is interested in developing the work in a particular direction, it is possible to reinforce this by intervening positively, e.g. providing a ransom note or a series of demands received from the terrorists. Instead of developing into an action-oriented 'hostage' drama, it is perfectly possible that from a starting point like this some classes might decide that the girl's disappearance was a purely domestic matter, to do with her relationship with her parents or caused by the influence of her friends. It is important for the teacher to be sensitive to the signals given by the class while interpreting the 'clues' as to the direction they are interested in pursuing.

disappearance, since a valuable necklace given to Anne by her father was still on her dressing-table. The pill bottle was open and empty. The message on the blackboard was what had been found scrawled on the dressing-table mirror in lipstick. What questions would the group like to ask?

The rest of this session consists entirely of the group questioning the teacher very closely and listening carefully to the answers which are given. In response to their questioning, it emerges that Anne's parents were recently divorced, that her father was a distinguished scientist who was attending a conference abroad at the time of her disappearance, and that she had been alone in the house with the housekeeper. The 'clues' are passed round the class and examined closely. Many searching questions are asked about the room, the possibilities of outsiders gaining entrance to the house, the various clues, particularly the pill bottle, the kind of girl Anne was, her friends, her relationship with the housekeeper, the existence of a boathouse nearby.

2   SOLUTIONS

The pupils begin to form hypotheses which include all the known clues.

The lesson ended with the class having formed a number of different opinions about the case. The teacher had succeeded in her objective of gaining the group's commitment and interest, and the pupils had listened intently throughout the lesson, both to the teacher and to each other.

In later lessons, developing this theme, the teacher's objectives were to encourage pupils to adopt different roles, and to begin to take responsibility for their own work. They interviewed various people connected with the case, with some of the pupils taking on these roles. In this case they eventually decided that the girl had been taken hostage by international terrorists. In the final sessions on this topic, they planned and carried out the rescue of the girl.

3   FURTHER DEVELOPMENTS

> Interviews with the girl's friends, teachers, parents, neighbours.
> Re-enacting the possible events of the night she disappeared.
> Examining the house and grounds for further evidence.
> Formally presenting this evidence and its implications to the police.
> An item on the girl's disappearance to be included in the 10 o'clock news.
> Holding a Press Conference about the case.
> Breaking the news of her disappearance to her parents.
> Going back in time to examine the motives, plans and purposes of Anne's captors.
> A list of the Terrorists' demands for the Press.
> As her captors, explaining to Anne why she has been taken hostage.
> Planning and carrying out the rescue attempt.
> Helping the hostage adjust to normal life after the rescue.

TEACHING NOTES

The potential problems posed by this group required that the teacher should focus her attention on them from the beginning of the session. Because of these problems, it was wise to write the 'advertisement' on the blackboard before the group entered the room. The teacher could then start immediately by reading the advertisement aloud to the group.

There was no need for an introductory discussion. In a topic like this, curiosity is a powerful factor in the group's response, whereas too much discussion can diffuse interest.

1   The class are seated in a circle. The teacher's role as Mrs Brown is very neutral at first. Her attitude seems very down-to-earth, and she insists that ghosts do not exist in the twentieth century. She hopes that, as sensible people, they do not believe in ghosts either. She rejects the stories told about the Manor as local superstition. When the group ask what is being said about the house, she refuses to go into details, as she says she does not wish to influence their minds in the wrong way. There is some laughter at this stage, and she joins in with it, while not giving up her role. Of course the locals are foolish and it is laughable to believe such nonsense. But although she does not admit that she believes in ghosts, she seems to be very unwilling to spend a night in the house. She explains that, like her uncle, she

7 The Haunted House

INTRODUCTORY LESSON

This lesson took place with a class of second years in a large classroom during a double period.

This was a class with problems of concentration, behavioural difficulties and limited social skills. They were unco-operative with each other and with their teachers. The teacher's objective was to unite the class in a common enquiry.

Preparation
Before the class enter the room, the teacher writes on the blackboard:

> £50
> offered to anyone who will spend one
> night in Darkwood Manor.
> Those interested please meet at
> The Swan Hotel at 6 p.m.

1 MRS BROWN'S OFFER

Whole group
The teacher introduces the work in role with a narrative link:
'My name is Mrs Brown. Thank you for coming here this evening. I'm pleased that so many of you have responded to my advertisement in the newspaper. I need your help.'
She goes on to explain why she has placed the advertisement in the newspaper. She has recently inherited the Manor from her uncle, who is dead. She is hoping to let or sell it. Unfortunately, she has discovered that there are so many unpleasant stories circulating about the house that she is totally unable to find any tenant or buyer who is prepared to take it on. She hopes that through the advertisement she will find some sensible, objective people who, after spending a night in the

suffers from a weak heart, and her doctor has advised her against any undue excitement.

Gradually, as the questioning proceeded, the group seemed increasingly unwilling to trust her. Their uncertainty about the house was transferred to fear and suspicion about Mrs Brown. They began to doubt her motives in wanting them to spend a night in the house.

During the questioning, the teacher as Mrs Brown tries to feed information gradually to the group. Details have not been decided in advance, but arise in response to questions. She does not burden them with too much informaton at any one time, and tries to build up the atmosphere as well as providing information. For example, when she is asked about the house, she tells them that if they will look out of the window they will be able to see the house, standing alone on top of the hill. As they can see, it is bleak and deserted, and in bad repair. It is obviously too big for her needs. She answers some questions evasively.

During this kind of session, it is important that the teacher should not be too dominant. A great deal of the information is in her hands, but she must allow the group to feel that they have a vital contribution to make to the work.

The teacher does not press the group into making a decision at this point. The longer the group take before entering the haunted house, the more likely it is that the eventual visit will be significant for them.

2*a*   These stories are told with a considerable sense of atmosphere, and with growing confidence and narrative skill by the group. Many of the 'visitors' are warned by the locals against going anywhere near the Manor.

b   The retelling of the stories is an enjoyable experience for the group. It allows the class to hear stories from each of the pairs and extends the sense of achieve-

house, will be prepared to sign a paper that there is nothing at all unusual about the house. She asks the group if they have any questions.

There follows a lengthy session in which the teacher in role as Mrs Brown is closely questioned by the group. Their questions focus on the following areas:

> What is the house like?
> Is there light and heat?
> Has Mrs Brown ever spent a night there?
> Does she mean to spend the night with the group in the house?
> How did her uncle die?
> What stories are being told about the house?
> Does she believe these stories?
> Can the group trust her to pay them the £50 if they accept her offer?
> Has anyone ever lived in the house apart from her uncle and his
>   housekeeper?

As well as responding to these questions, Mrs Brown also questions the group along the following lines:

> Are any of the group already experienced in investigations of this kind?
> What preparations will they make for spending the night in the Manor?
> Will they take equipment such as cameras and tape-recorders with them?
> Have they already spoken to the local people?
> Do any of them believe in ghosts?
> Will they be prepared to sign a paper freeing Mrs Brown from all
>   responsibility for anything which may happen to them while they are in
>   her house?
> What are the names of their next of kin?

After this session, some of the group are still undecided about the wisdom of accepting Mrs Brown's offer. She suggests that they should wait and think about it carefully before making their decision.

2   STRANGE HAPPENINGS

a   *In pairs*
The teacher asks one person in each pair to be a newcomer to the village – perhaps one of the people who were present at the previous meeting. The other person is a local resident. What tales does the local person know about the Manor house? How much are they prepared to tell the visitor?

b   *Whole group*
The pupils who were the visitors in the previous pair work now retell the stories they were told to the whole group. These tales are very varied, including ghosts of

ment felt by the original story-tellers. The fact that the stories may be varied and inconsistent should not be a difficulty. Each should be accepted, not necessarily as the truth about the Manor, but as an example of the horrifying rumours which are prevalent about the house.

3   The previous work has provided motivation for this discussion. If the subsequent work is to have any depth, it is important that the pupils begin to alter the level of their thinking.

[The self-discipline required in encountering the ghost was useful to this group. Focusing on the problems of making contact with an uneasy spirit gradually made the experience of visiting the haunted house less superficially 'scary'. They became very inventive in helping the ghost to find its baby. Perhaps the most valuable part of this exercise came in the written work done by the group after the drama was over. They eagerly wrote the history of the house, and accounts of their meeting with the ghost, as well as producing some interesting art work.]

The starting-point provided atmosphere, provoked curiosity, and involved the group together in the same investigation. It may be necessary for the teacher to slow up the work, so that when the group visit the Manor, their presence there has acquired significance. There may be difficulty in maintaining tension, and making sure that the night in the haunted house is as significant in fact as in anticipation.

many kinds, as well as werewolves and vampires. Mrs Brown accepts these stories as the kind of tales which are told about the house, but insists that they are all without foundation.

3   DISCUSSION

The session finishes with a discussion about the nature of ghosts. If they do exist, what are they? Are their intentions always evil? Why might a ghost want to make contact with the world of the living?
[This group continued to work enthusiastically on this theme, and in a subsequent session they entered the house and encountered a ghost, played by another teacher. Their tendency to scream and giggle was counteracted by the ghost, who was so pathetic and timid that they had to be very quiet and sensitive in order not to frighten it away. Finally, after several visits to the house, they learned that the ghost had lost its baby in a fire many centuries before. Could they help the uneasy spirit to find rest?]
   This kind of first session can provide an intriguing start to work in drama, especially for an unmotivated class. Although the subject may seem excessively plot-oriented – 'What will happen when we enter the haunted house?' – it is really based on enquiry. The *past* happenings in the house are as important to consider as what will happen in the future. It is probable that no two groups will develop the work in the same way, from this kind of starting-point.

4   FURTHER DEVELOPMENTS

Making a list of the people in the village who might have access to *facts* about the Manor. For example, the doctor, the constable, the oldest inhabitant, a relation of the housekeeper, the vicar, the innkeeper.
Interviewing these people. (Members of the group might take on some of these roles, and be interviewed by the rest of the class.)
Showing the troubled history of the house over the centuries by presenting brief rehearsed scenes or tableaux.
Visting the Manor house by daylight, and making a thorough examination of the place.
Listing evidence which has been found.
Carrying out a ritual or ceremony which might put to rest any unquiet spirits.
A dance-drama which shows the meeting of ghosts and humans.
The nightmare of the night in the haunted house.
Discovering that the Manor house is not haunted, but deciding to open it to the public as a typical 'haunted house'. How could frightening effects be created by the group?

TEACHING NOTES

The teacher occasionally hands over the responsibility of choice to the class and tests their response to this kind of initiative. In this instance he wants to start from material in which they have a strong interest since he hopes to extend the theme beyond a single lesson. Many groups may not be prepared to take such decisions and teachers may put them very much at risk in expecting them to do so. An alternative course of action might be to sound out possible topics and interests at the end of the previous session with the class. This will allow time to plan opening strategies in advance.

1*a*   The teacher reminds the groups that they will need to decide on the incident, the location and the characters involved, as well as on the best ways of presenting their scene to an audience. In other words, 'What, where, who and how?'

   b   In work of this kind it may be useful and indeed necessary to build in certain controls which help pupils to cope with the rapid and often violent nature of the action. Though it was not necessary in this instance, the teacher will often use a 'freeze-frame' technique which breaks a sequence of activity into still-life tableaux moving from one frame to the next on a given signal. It could have been used here to stylize the sequences concerning the discovery of the theft and the subsequent chase.

8 *Young Offenders*

This lesson took place with a third-year class in a classroom for a double period. The teacher's objective was to help this class to extend their work from the kind of drama with which they were most familiar – preparing scenes which they showed to the rest of the class – by developing one topic over several lessons.

Introduction
The teacher asked the class if *they* would like to suggest a topic for some new work in drama. After a short discussion they decided that their starting-point should be 'something to do with teenage crime'. They would work in small groups. Each group would prepare and present a situation which would show how the crime was committed.

A space was cleared by moving desks and chairs to one side of the room.

1   THE CRIME

Small groups
  a   The groups begin to plan their scenes. In each of these cases the crime to be shown involved a theft of some kind. The teacher sets a ten-minute time-limit for this stage of the activity and moves among the groups giving advice where it is needed.
  b   In turn, the groups present their scenes to the rest of the class. The teacher introduces the scenes as examples of the kind of teenage crime which frequently occurs, and indicates that later on he would like the pupils to investigate why such crimes take place.
This group chose to show:
  i   Two members of a schoolboy gang stealing items from a newsagent's shop while two others divert the proprietor's attention.
  ii   An incident similar to the above in nearly all respects except that the theft took place in a record store.

2   Some classes do not regard discussion as an important part of the drama lesson. They are concerned only to move from one activity to the next. It may take some time for the teacher to introduce them to the idea that they themselves can take considerable responsibility for determining the future development of the work through discussion of this kind.

3   The pupils give grudging assent to this suggestion. This is the point where they sometimes refuse to move forward and develop the material. On this occasion the teacher gives them little opportunity to voice any objections. He moves quickly into the next stage of the work.

It is not necessary for the room to be arranged in such a way that it constitutes an authentic representation of a police station. What matters is that the pupils feel it to be appropriate to their idea of such a setting and to the task in hand.

The teacher constantly refers to the work they have just done. All subsequent investigations will be very much based on their presentations. He reads out each summary once it is written up.

The teacher does not indicate in advance that he will work in role but simply begins to talk of 'this' police station rather than 'that' one. Thus he indicates in language and action that he too is moving into the fictional context.

4   The teacher uses his role to organize this activity. This kind of intervention may

iii   A gang operating in a busy shopping street staging a diversion while some of its members 'lift' wallets and purses from the bystanders.

2   DISCUSSION

Whole group

Each presentation lasts no more than a few minutes and the observers' comments are related almost entirely to the manner of performance. The teacher attempts to initiate discussion on the content of the scene but gets little response. The pupils are not concerned to talk about *what* has been shown but about *how* it has been done. Only very slowly does the teacher begin to get a response to such questions as 'Why do you think these teenagers are doing this?' and 'How can we set up some drama to help us find out the reasons for their actions?'

3   AT THE POLICE STATION

Whole group

The teacher asks the group if they will use the scenes they have presented and take the work a stage further by exploring what would happen if the teenagers who were involved in the thefts were to get caught.

The suspects remain in their roles as do the shopkeepers who were robbed and the passers-by who had money taken. The remaining pupils are asked to adopt the roles of police who will interview the suspects, victims and witnesses at the local police station. There is an equal number of interviewers and interviewees.

The teacher asks the class to set up the room in a way which will be appropriate for conducting the interviews. The pupils decide to arrange separate 'rooms', each one containing a desk and two chairs.

The teacher reminds the station staff of the incidents which have occurred and of the people who will be brought in for questioning. He writes a brief summary of each alleged crime on the blackboard, and the pupils provide relevant details of time, place, and the names of those involved. The members of the station staff are each given a piece of paper and a pencil. They are asked to choose whom they will interview and then to write down a list of the questions which it will be important to ask. They move off to their 'rooms'.

The suspects and witnesses are told to wait in separate corners of the classroom. They will be called for questioning when the police station staff are ready.

The teacher now adopts a role as a senior member of the station staff. This permits him to move between the groups, remind the suspects of their rights under the law and assist the station staff in the task of preparing their questions.

4   INTERVIEWS

In pairs

During the course of the interviews the teacher (in role) moves from one pair to

be helpful in reminding pupils of the seriousness of the task and will provide a valuable means of supporting those pupils who have run out of questions to ask. Once again, the teacher's role gives him access to the drama and enables him to assist in building the make-believe.

The class may find the device of spotlighting interviews cumbersome. It may be difficult for them to switch from being observers to carrying on their conversations in pairs, and *vice versa*.

5   Any additional information which has been gained from the interviews can be written up on the board to accompany the brief summary of each incident. The discussion could also be conducted in role with the station staff reviewing the progress of the investigations before returning to the task of interviewing suspects and others connected with the cases.

There may be cases of conflicting evidence. The pupils can ask for the initial scenes to be replayed so that they can look again at what happened. The teacher then explains that each person involved will have seen the incident differently and that some people may be concerned to misrepresent the events, but if the 'station staff' agree to revert to their original roles then this replaying might provide a good starting-point for the next lesson.

The pupils reconstruct the events which have brought an individual to this particular situation. What are the reasons which have led him or her to this criminal act?

another, supporting those who may be having difficulties, asking additional questions which may put greater pressure on suspects, and sympathizing with or challenging witnesses. He occasionally asks individual members of the station staff to withdraw from the 'interview room' in order to strengthen their commitment to their new roles by asking them how the interview is proceeding and by suggesting alternative lines of questioning.

The teacher finally brings the interviews to a close and explains that he would like the whole group to hear what is being said in each of the 'rooms'. He asks the pupils to accept a convention whereby all the pairs will continue their conversations until, at a given signal (for example, a hand-clap), the interviews will stop and the teacher will point to just one pair who will continue their dialogue. The rest of the class will become observers. Another hand-clap will indicate that the others then resume their interviews until a similar signal is given for a different pair to take over.

5   REPORTING BACK

Whole group

Out of role, the teacher asks the group members to report on their findings. He wants to know if there are leads which should be followed and if there are other people who should be interviewed in connection with each case.

It may be an idea to 'replay' some of the incidents while the observers take written notes of what they have witnessed. These can be used later in discussion to examine the way in which eye-witness accounts agree or differ.

The pupils may also freeze the action of each scene and question those involved about their motives and their thoughts at that particular moment. The teacher can use this replaying as an opportunity to point out how presentational work can be made more effective and also lead on to other forms of enquiry.

FURTHER DEVELOPMENTS

These might include interviewing the parents, friends and teachers of the accused. Or setting up small-group scenes which show aspects of the suspect's life, any previous criminal incidents in which he or she may have been involved, and relationships with parents and school. It may be possible to focus on just one of the original gang members. In each group this character could be represented by a different person.

Alternatively, the exercise could be set up with the whole group seated in a circle, volunteers being called on to act out the kinds of situations indicated above. Additional characters could be introduced into the action when necessary. At some points it may be possible to involve the whole group – for example when the central character meets his friends at the youth club.

6   Strictly speaking, most cases involving young people will be heard only by magistrates in the juvenile court (see following notes). For the purposes of the drama, we have taken some licence by suggesting that they be brought before a higher court and so provide for a greater variety of roles and a more elaborate dramatic procedure.

Some pupils may also like to prepare other cases which can be brought before the court. The background to such cases might be examined by using approaches similar to those outlined in this lesson — showing the incident, and interviewing those involved in the case.

NOTE ON JUVENILE COURTS

These are often held in an ordinary room, not a courtroom, with the magistrates seated at a table. They hear the cases of young people between the ages of ten and seventeen. A panel of juvenile court magistrates consists of not more than three justices and must include one man and one woman.

The accused may be represented by a lawyer or the case may be put by a parent or friend. The court is not open to the public. The press may attend but must not print the name of any child (whether offender or witness) or any facts which might reveal the identity of the person appearing before the court.

Procedure

1   The charge is read out by the clerk of the court.
2   A lawyer outlines the case for the prosecution and calls any witnesses.
3   These may be cross-questioned by the person representing the defendant.
4   Witnesses may be called in support of the defendant.
5   The defendant is asked to make a statement or give evidence on oath.
6   The magistrates decide on their verdict.

They may wish to make a care order. Other possibilities include fines, supervision orders and recommendations of Borstal treatment for serious or persistent offenders.

6 BRINGING THE SUSPECTS TO TRIAL

This will require a certain amount of prior planning since the court-room procedures involved can often pose problems for the smooth running of the drama. If some pupils are not prepared to take a very active role they may be given the chance to work as members of the public, court ushers or in the press gallery, perhaps preparing newspaper reports of the case.

NOTE ON MAGISTRATES' COURTS AND CROWN COURTS

All adult criminal cases will have a preliminary hearing in a magistrates' court; the most serious will be referred to the crown courts. There must be at least two and not more than seven magistrates on the bench of a magistrates' court. Cases in the crown court are tried in the presence of a judge and jury.

As an aid to achieving some accuracy in the simulation of crown court procedure, the main points are summarized below.

1 Jury is selected by ballot from those called for jury service; the defendant has the right to object to up to three jurors without stating any reason.

2 The twelve members of the jury are sworn in by the clerk of the court. The Christian oath is as follows:
'I swear by almighty God that I will faithfully try the several issues joined between our Sovereign Lady the Queen and the Defendant and give a true verdict according to the evidence.'

3 The charge is read out by the Clerk and the plea taken ('Guilty' or 'Not guilty').

4 Details of the case are described by the counsel for the Prosecution.

5 The Prosecution calls and examines prosecution witnesses, who may subsequently be cross-examined by the counsel for the Defence. Prosecution may then re-examine.

6 Counsel for the Prosecution closes the case.

7 Counsel for the Defence calls and questions the defendant and defence witnesses. These may be cross-examined by the Prosecution. Defence may then re-examine.

8 Summing up by Prosecution, by Defence and by the judge.

9 Jury retires to consider the verdict; they are escorted by the court usher to the jury room.

10 Judge hears the verdict.
Clerk: Members of the jury, have you agreed upon a verdict?
     (*Response*)
Clerk: Do you find the defendant guilty or not guilty?
     (*Response*)
The judge then passes sentence where appropriate.

TEACHING NOTES

This kind of theme is often chosen by the pupils, since it suggests action and excitement. If the theme is tackled directly, the work is likely to be superficial and lacking in integrity of thought or feeling. While the pupils may enjoy the excitement of the crisis they may lack satisfaction at any deeper level, and are likely to be *demonstrating* obvious panic, fear and loss rather than really experiencing these feelings in any way. If the teacher can approach the theme so that the implications and consequences of the disaster are considered, the work may achieve greater depth and give the pupils greater satisfaction.

1   The teacher uses narration to introduce the work, so that a common context is established. It is also a secure way of starting with a class who are not accustomed to working as a whole group, or working with the teacher in role.

2   This class chose to show different aspects of the disaster. If they had decided to

9 Disaster

This lesson took place with a third-year class in a drama room during a double period.

This class was accustomed to working in small groups on their own improvised plays. The teacher's objective was to involve them in work which would encourage them to tackle a subject as a whole class, but would allow them to use their experience of small-group work and build on the satisfactions which they found in this kind of approach. They had asked to work on the theme of 'Disaster'.

1 DISASTER

The teacher begins the work with a piece of narration:
'Twenty-five years ago, in a certain community, a terrible disaster occurred. The way of life of that community was changed forever. The young people of the community who had been born after the disaster decide to commemorate the twenty-fifth anniversary by presenting a play about the disaster. They hope that this will remind people of what happened, and will prevent such a disaster from ever happening again.'

Here the teacher stops, and in discussion the pupils make up their minds about the kind of disaster which had happened to the community. They consider natural disasters, such as floods and earthquakes, but in this case decide that a man-made disaster will be more interesting to explore. Such an occurrence might lead to disasters in the natural world as well. They agree that this disaster was a nuclear explosion, not due to war, but a result of a series of blunders on the part of the government. It leads to great devastation and changes in the environment. The drama will be set some time in the future.

2 THE CAUSE OF THE DISASTER

Small groups
The teacher asks the class to get into small groups. Can they prepare a short scene

present the same scene in a variety of ways this would also have been useful, since it would have allowed speculation on which version of the event was the most accurate, and how conflicting accounts of the disaster had developed.

3*a*   The role taken by the teacher is extremely close to her real role as teacher. Her attitude is that the class are young people and she is an adult in authority over them. The role is apparently very sympathetic and understanding on the surface, but there is the awareness that power lies behind it.

b   The role here becomes very close to that of teacher — the adult who knows best, and who expects that her useful suggestions will be adopted. The teacher is hoping that this increasingly overbearing attitude will prompt the class to oppose her, and so will increase their commitment to their own work. As the pupils are unused to working in this way, it takes some time for them to realize that the 'rules of the game' allow them to respond negatively to the suggestions made by the teacher in role.

This class were not sufficiently accustomed to working together as one group to be able to continue this kind of discussion in role for too long. The teacher decided to continue the discussion out of role in order to clarify the situation, and allow for the consideration of alternative ideas.

The teacher does not allow the discussion to continue so long that everything about the society is made explicit. She wants the class to continue to make decisions and discoveries in the drama.

which will demonstrate how the disaster came to happen? One group decides to show the lead-up to the event – the desire for nuclear supremacy and political power, and the fear of other nations.

Another group shows the actual moment of the catastrophe. A third group shows a scene after the disaster in which the government try to blame what happened on individual carelessness, and to cover up the real culprits.

The teacher asks the groups to play their scenes one after the other, without pausing for comment between them.

3 THE STATE COUNCILLOR

a *Whole group*

Next, the teacher calls the class together formally and asks them to sit in a circle. She takes on the role of a visitor from the State Council for the Arts, and tells them that she is very pleased that they are working so hard to commemorate this tragic incident in their history. She admires their talent, as well as their effort and dedication. However, she is slightly unhappy about the way they have chosen to approach their task. They seem to be taking a rather negative and depressing view of the whole incident. They also seem to have got their facts wrong. She tells them that it is now known that the disaster was due to the sabotage of one employee, who had become unbalanced due to overwork. There was nothing sinister about the disaster. It was the result of the unfortunate actions of one well-meaning but disturbed individual.

b *Questions and discussions*

At this point the pupils begin to question her, but she insists that as they cannot know the full facts, they must take her word for it. She suggests that they do a play which represents a positive look at the way in which their society coped with the disaster, and the way in which they have rebuilt the community. Alternatively, they might like to present for the commemoration a classic play, such as *Romeo and Juliet*. This would be a positive link with the best traditions of the past. The pupils begin to object to her suggestions, but she continues to be very persuasive. If they will accept her ideas and change their play, the State Council for the Arts will give them a great deal of support, including the use of a new theatre for young people, which they will be asked to organize. She asks them to consider her offer very seriously, and leaves the group.

The class continue to discuss her suggestions for several minutes, still in the attitudes of the young people presenting the play. The teacher interrupts this discussion after some minutes, in order to clarify the situation.

Next, in discussion out of role, the class decide what has happened to the society they belong to in the years since the disaster. Using the visit of the teacher in role as a clue, they decide that the society has become very repressive, and as a result of the devastation of the environment, everybody now lives underground.

4   Because these small-group plays are feeding into the central theme, the groups watch each other's work with interest and concentration. They need the information which each group's scene contains in order to construct a picture of the society in which they live.

The checklist reinforces the effect of the group plays, and focuses the attention of the class on the *qualities* of the scene and the information it contains. This is also a useful vocabulary exercise, and one which emphasizes that the work is being shared. In discussion at the end of these scenes, any inconsistencies and difficulties are ironed out.

5   This may not be an exercise which many classes will find easy to carry out, but the teacher includes it in order to give the class experience of yet another way of working. She stresses that this may look like a speeded-up film, which allows any embarrassment from the class to dissipate in rapid physical activity, and some laughter. The mood can be helped by playing a piece of electronic music, and reducing the level of light in the room. The exercise also reinforces the mechanical and regimented nature of the society which they are attempting to represent.

4   ASPECTS OF THE PRESENT SOCIETY

Small groups

Working in their small groups, the teacher asks the class to show various aspects of the society they live in, which will reveal how it has developed since the disaster. Each group is asked to focus on a different aspect of the society – for example, family life, law and order, education, leisure, health, the military.

The groups prepare and show their work, and the picture which emerges is of an extremely repressive and highly ordered society, where friendship and feeling are discouraged, and in which criticism or free speech is not permitted. As each group shows its work, the teacher asks the rest of the class to provide single words or phrases which will describe what they have seen. These are listed on the blackboard, and act as a checklist to remind the class of what they have built up so far.

5   A DAY IN THE LIFE

Individual work

Using the information provided by the previous scenes, the teacher asks every pupil to live through one day in this society. This will be a movement exercise, extremely speeded up, in which the individual makes no contact with anyone else in the class.

The first session ended at this point. The teacher's objectives for the lesson had been achieved, and the class were beginning to realize that the scope of their work might be enlarged by engaging in a shared context. They were very keen to continue work on the theme, and did not express frustration that their experience of 'Disaster' had been limited.

FURTHER DEVELOPMENTS

These might include:

> In pairs, discussing with a friend what they have heard about life before the disaster.
> Interviewing elderly people who were alive then and remember what life used to be like.
> In groups, a visit to the surface of the planet.
> In groups, showing what life is like on the surface.
> A confrontation with the authorities about the play they intend to present.
> Attempts to change the society they live in.

TEACHING NOTES

At six o'clock on the Saturday evening, the two doctors returned. I again refused to take food out of the cup and resisted their efforts to make me take it. Then they tried to force tubes into my nostrils. There seemed to be something sharp at the end of these tubes and I felt a sharp pricking sensation . . . it appeared that the nasal passage was closed. . . . I was raised into a sitting position and a tube about two feet long was produced. My mouth was prised open with what felt like a steel instrument and then I felt them feeling for the proper passage. All this time I was held down by four or five wardresses. I felt a choking sensation and what I judged to be a cork gag was placed between my teeth to keep my mouth open. It was a horrible feeling altogether. I experienced great sickness, especially when the tube was being withdrawn.

Laura Ainsworth quoted in *The Militant Suffragettes*

The teacher knew that the members of this group were capable of working well together and were skilled at presenting small-group scenes.

1a   The teacher suggests a time-limit of thirty minutes for the planning, preparation and revision of the scenes. In practice this was extended by another ten minutes or so.

The teacher was occasionally asked to provide historical information, but very rarely needed to make any points about presentational matters. If working with pupils who do not possess either the social or dramatic skills exhibited by this particular group, then the teacher will need to offer much more help in the task of translating ideas into dramatic form.

b   At this point they asked if they could wear the full-length practice skirts kept in the drama room props cupboard. Costume seemed to help them adopt an appropriate style of movement and gesture.

10 *Suffragettes*

This lesson took place with a group of fourth-year girls working in the drama studio for a double period.

They had asked to do some drama on the suffragettes since they were studying the topic as part of their history course. In response to the teacher's questioning they begin to talk about the women themselves, the reasons which prompted them to take up the cause, the kind of opposition they had to face and the actions they took in order to achieve their goals. The teacher asks them to think about the counter-arguments that would be used by women who were not in favour of the suffragettes' proposals. These are the attitudes she would like the girls to use as a starting-point for the drama.

1 THE MEETING OF THE LADIES' GUILD

a The class divides into two groups. Each group is asked to prepare a short playlet which will be presented at a meeting of a small village Ladies' Guild in the year 1900. The title of the piece to be performed is 'A Woman's Place'.

The brief is given to this group in confidence. The teacher wants the contents of their play to come as a complete surprise to the audience.

The two groups begin their preparation, but the teacher asks one group to adopt a potentially controversial viewpoint. They will represent visitors from a neighbouring community. They have been greatly influenced by friends recently returned from the city with radical ideas about the place of women in society. They will use their play to communicate this point of view.

b The Ladies' Guild holds its half-yearly meeting. They are fortunate in having the vicar's wife in attendance.

The teacher explains that she will be working in role as the vicar's wife. At her gracious invitation, the meeting is to be held at the vicarage. She asks the class to accept that one group will be visitors to the village. The residents' group will therefore need to welcome the guests.

c   The presentation of the plays will be set within the framework of the drama. They are put into a context which lends both motivation and purpose to the performance.

Although both plays may present stereotyped situations and reactions, this is totally in keeping with their nature as propaganda pieces. Each has a clearly-defined message and stock characters. The teacher draws attention to this fact in the final discussion.

Throughout this lengthy section, the girls remained very firmly committed to the kind of attitudes which each group had been asked to represent. The teacher may have to deal with some anachronisms at the end of the lesson. For the moment she is content to let them pass in order not to destroy the seriousness which the girls bring to the situation.

2   A project of this nature may involve the teacher and pupils in further research. Where the teacher is unsure of the historical information, she may need to ask the girls to accept what they already know as a basis for continuing the drama. The facts can be checked later. She offers information as and when it becomes necessary.

The girls in this group chose to follow the fortunes of a small number of young women, each of whom took up a similar course of action to that pursued by the main character in the second playlet.

3b   The WSPU was founded by Mrs Emmeline Pankhurst and her daughter Christabel in 1903. The members pledged to campaign for their cause with a greater militancy than had previously been shown by the suffrage movement. Their policy was to admit women only and to be independent of any political party, though there were close connections with the Independent Labour Party and its leader James Keir Hardie. The WSPU opened its official headquarters in London in 1906.

In pairs, the girls could be asked to show to the meeting the kind of situations that arise when a member of the WSPU tries to persuade another woman to join the movement.

The village ladies take up positions where they will be ready to welcome their visitors. The vicar's wife waits with them. The guests enter the 'vicarage' and are made welcome. The vicar's wife asks the residents if they will perform their play first. She is sure that it will be a pleasurable and uplifting afternoon.

c The first offering presents a number of situations in which wives and daughters are fully obedient to male commands. The players make frequent asides to the audience in which they confirm their pleasure in serving their menfolk. They warn against the spread of ideas challenging the *status quo*. The vicar's wife leads the (muted) applause, expresses her complete agreement with the sentiments of the piece and praises the performers.

The visitors then present their play. The central character is a young girl who defies the wishes of her parents and fiancé in order to seek a better education. She becomes a strong advocate of women's suffrage and asks the members of the audience to lend their support to the campaign. They are horrified by these sentiments and voice their disapproval. The argument becomes heated and the meeting breaks up. The village residents are deeply offended and the vicar's wife asks the visitors to leave. After further argument they reluctantly agree to do so.

2 DISCUSSION

The drama is brought to a close at this point and the girls discuss the issues raised by the conflicting opinions seen in the two plays. They talk of the difficulties faced by those who sought to change prevailing attitudes and of the limited options available to them.

The teacher asks how they would like to pursue the theme in future lessons and subsequently sets up the following activities in order to develop the drama.

3 FURTHER DEVELOPMENTS

a In small groups the pupils prepare a scene which will show how a young woman tells her family of her decision to support the campaign for women's suffrage. Whom does she tell first? What is their reaction? Does it mean that the girl will be forced to break with her family and friends? What opposition is put in her way?

b The pupils represent young women who have become members of the WSPU (Women's Social and Political Union). They have organized a meeting to talk about the kind of changes they hope to achieve. They confirm their support for each other and pledge that they will remain united and strong in the face of criticism.

What backgrounds do these women come from? Are there any who will be prepared to speak of the particular sacrifices they made? Have any of them found difficulty in enlisting the support of other women, particularly from amongst the working class?

c   The teacher takes on the role of the MP (male) or asks a member of the group, another member of staff, a student or an older pupil to do so. Other members of the girl's family may also need to be portrayed, as well as neighbours, passers-by etc.

d   This exercise could be set up as a series of individual monologues or be used as the basis for pair-work activities in which the prisoner justifies her actions to a visitor.

e   The observers may question the individuals in the photograph.

f   Some of the pupils can be asked to change roles and represent the Governor and committee members. The prisoners are brought to the prison office for interview. The interviewers sit behind the table and the prisoners stand in front of them. The other prisoners are not present though they can be ranged around the room in their cells (i.e. on their chairs.)

g   This strategy works best if the teacher can enlist the help of four or five pupils from another group in order to role-play her aides in the demonstration. She will be setting up a piece of theatre for the class and so that they can all share in the same experience it is desirable for them all to remain as observers. Both this and the subsequent activity need to be informed with as much accurate, grisly detail as possible.

The physical details of the process need to be obscured as much as possible by the group of aides crowded into a circle around the 'prisoner'. The effectiveness of the exercise is more likely to be achieved by the demonstrator's graphic commentary. Occasional actions can be made visible, e.g. the teacher holding up the gag for all to see before, apparently, wedging it in the prisoner's mouth.

h   The teacher will need to take some care in choosing a pupil to represent the prisoner who is being fed since her co-operation and skill will be essential to the success of this particular strategy. She will be helping to create a vivid experience for the listeners. Though she will be held down by the aides, each detail of the feeding will obviously be done only verbally.

If the prisoners vow to carry on their campaign, the teacher can narrate them through the hardships and indignities suffered by this small group. It will not be

c   One of the suffragettes is the daughter of a prominent politician who has promised to support the passage of a Bill advocating votes for women. He has reneged on this promise. With a group of friends, the young woman decides to revisit her home and cause a disturbance which will put him to shame and publicize their cause.

The girls set up the room to represent the entrance to the family house and the street outside. They plan their demonstration and the slogans they will use. This planning is not revealed to the MP and family.

What arguments might the father use to win back his daughter? How will she reply? What is the outcome of the demonstration?

d   The suffragettes have been put in prison for their violent action against property. In their cells each one writes a letter to a sympathetic friend.

e   In small groups, the pupils prepare a series of 'photographs' which they show to the others. Each one illustrates the kind of activities that members of the WSPU are engaged in as a means of publicizing their cause. For example, marches, demonstrations, arson, window breaking, stone-throwing, interrupting public meetings and political debates, organizing processions and pageants etc.

f   One by one the prisoners are brought before the Governor (and a committee?). They will be granted some remission of sentence if they are prepared to admit the foolishness of their actions and make a promise not to involve themselves in a similar activities in the future.

g   The prisoners have elected to go on hunger strike in order to gain further publicity for their cause.

The teacher works in role either as doctor or governor and sets up a demonstration of force-feeding techniques for a group of prison nurses/wardresses. Some of the prisoners are now so weak that they must be forcibly fed in order to prevent their death and subsequent martyrdom. The demonstration is set up in the centre of the room. The prisoners watch and listen from their cells.

On this occasion a full-size, costumed tailor's dummy was used to represent the prisoner. Some of the feeding instruments were also used, namely an enamel bowl, a funnel, a long piece of rubber tubing and a piece of wood serving as a gag.

h   The force-feeding begins. Each prisoner can be given a final chance to take some food. Those who agree to do so can be removed to another 'cell' and watch what happens from there.

One of the remaining inmates is brought from her chair to the centre of the room. The other prisoners are placed on their chairs facing away from the centre. They will be able to hear what goes on since the order is given for all cell doors to be left open.

The doctor and aides crowd around the prisoner in a tight circle. The process of force-feeding is described in detail as if it was actually being carried out on the person in the middle. Afterwards she is taken back to her cell. The prisoners are

necessary for the force-feeding to be repeated with each pupil unless the teacher feels that the effectiveness of the experience is likely to be increased by such repetition.

k   1918   Representation of the People Act gave the vote to women over the age of 30.
    1928   Equal Franchise Act gave equal voting rights to all men and women over the age of 21.

brought before the committee and asked if they now wish to change their minds about continuing the hunger-strike.

In small groups, they may be given the chance to talk things through with their friends and provide mutual support, comfort and reassurance to those who feel they want to give up.

i Released from prison and now resting in a hostel, the suffragettes are visited by women from other countries who are sympathetic to their cause. In pairs, the ex-prisoners talk to their visitors about their experiences.

j A number of WSPU members meet to conduct a private memorial service in memory of their colleague Emily Davison who has thrown herself under the king's horse at the 1913 Derby. Their contributions take a variety of forms: poems, songs, playlets, personal reminiscences. The items are linked together by the teacher or the members of the group.

k In pairs, a suffragette is reconciled with one of her parents or an estranged friend. It is some time after women have been granted the vote. In view of the fact that this was not granted as a direct result of the suffrage movement do they still feel that their fight was worthwhile? What did it achieve?

FURTHER READING

BBC Publications, *Shoulder to Shoulder*, 1974

Lewenbank, Sheila, *Women and Trade Unions*, 1977

Pankhurt, Emmeline, *My Own Story*, Eveleigh Nash, 1914

Pankhurst, Sylvia, *The Suffragette Movement*, reprinted Virago, 1977

Raeburn, Antonia, *The Militant Suffragettes*, Michael Joseph, 1973

Rooke, Patrick, *Women's Rights*, Wayland, 1972

Rosen, Andrew, *Rise Up, Women*, Routledge & Kegan Paul, 1974

Schools Council History Project, 13–16, *The Suffragette Derby of 1913*, Holmes McDougall, 1976

Snellgrove, L. E., *Suffragettes and the Votes for Women*, Then and There series, Longman, 1964

Strachey, Ray, *The Cause*, reprinted Cedric Chivers, 1974

TEACHING NOTES

Many of the strategies outlined in this lesson plan bear obvious similarities to those illustrated at greater length in an earlier section: 'The Way West'. Though specific events and situations are not common to the two structures, both deal with the same kind of theme: people who choose or who are forced to leave their homes in search of a better life elsewhere.

The teacher elects to 'distance' potentially controversial material by placing it within an historical context.

Factual background

Between 1860 and 1914 roughly 25 million Europeans settled in the United States of America. In the early stages immigrants came from North-west Europe, principally from Germany, Ireland, Britain and Scandinavia. The majority were from farming backgrounds and were suffering from the effects of rapid technological change and the threat of competition from new food-growing areas. Some were skilled industrial workers attracted by the high wages on offer. Later on the migrants were joined by people from Eastern and Southern Europe and from the Middle East. Many of these groups faced similar economic hardship though some of them left because they were deeply dissatisfied with political conditions.

The vast majority of the newcomers settled in the cities. They looked for work in the factories and small businesses of the thriving urban areas. They also sought close contact with fellow countrymen and organized special societies for mutual support both against the growing hostility from certain sections of the community and against the squalid conditions in which they were forced to live.

1   The outline of the cards should be prepared in advance by the teacher. They ask for a number of details: Name? Age? Occupation? Country of origin? Destination in America? Have you a job to go to? If so, what is it? Have you any relatives living there already? If so, give details. Reasons for leaving home country?

11 *Emigrants*

This lesson took place with a third-year group working in the drama room for a double period of sixty minutes.

Objectives
The teacher wanted to set up some drama that would help pupils to look at the motives which underlie people's decisions to leave their homeland and seek a new life in another country. They would examine the kind of problems faced by people in this situation. The drama was to be set within a particular historical context.

Preparation
The teacher asks the pupils to name the reasons which might make people want to leave their own country and make their home elsewhere. They see the major ones as being concerned with lack of opportunity, financial hardship, persecution of various kinds and the pursuit of better living conditions. The teacher says that these are exactly the kind of reasons that he wants to focus on as a starting-point for the drama. He gives them a brief description of the causes underlying the massive movement of people from Europe to America at the turn of the century and draws a rough sketch-map on the board to illustrate the areas where the emigrants came from.

1 IDENTITY CARDS

Small groups
The teacher asks each pupil to fill in an identity card. These will help them to start thinking about the kind of roles they will need to adopt in order to start the drama: they are people leaving Europe in the year 1900; they are travelling to America to seek a better life.

The teacher sets this task as a way of helping pupils to build their roles. They do not necessarily have to remain faithful to these first identities. The teacher is more concerned to get them thinking about *the kind of people* who made this journey rather than involve them in detailed character-building.

It may be sensible to put certain restrictions on the age ranges permitted; the attempt of a thirteen-year-old to play a toddler or octogenarian can distract from the real purpose of the theme.

2   During the course of getting used to the new environment, issues may arise which can lead to a productive line of enquiry either at this point or later in the lesson. It is impossible to predict these in advance so teachers will have to assess their dramatic potential on the spot.

a   These pupils are encouraged to ask questions and to seek out the information they consider relevant. Any questions that cannot be answered can be held for reference to a higher unseen authority.

NB It is important for the teacher not to be in a role which suggests absolute command. He is a go-between.

b   The pupils found it difficult to carry out this task and were unable to agree on a final list of representatives. The teacher intervened and set up a different activity.

e   The task is designed to get the members of the group interacting with each other, but pupils may not be ready to lend themselves to a large-group discussion at this stage in the proceedings. They may still be occupied with working out their own concerns: arranging their living quarters, making friends with neighbours, etc.

The pupils can work together as members of a family group or they can remain as individuals who are making the journey alone. He reminds them that they are not wealthy and that they will have had to save hard to raise the price of the fare. They are to keep their identity cards with them at all times.

2   IN STEERAGE

Whole group

Teacher and pupils move the chairs to form a square in the centre of the room. It is a very confined space. This will represent the steerage quarters of a ship *en route* from Europe to New York.

a   The teacher tells the class that he will start the drama by working in role as one of the ship's officers. He will be responsible for bringing them on board and settling them into their places. Are there any questions before they begin? The pupils ask if they have already paid for their tickets, how much it has cost them and how long the journey will take. The teacher says that all other information will be given on board.

b   The emigrants stand next to those people with whom they will be making the journey and take up a position around the sides of the room. They pose for a 'circular photograph'; it is as if there is a camera in the middle of the room which slowly revolves and captures an image of each group waiting patiently to start the voyage.

c   They take their places and the teacher stands in the centre of the circle. He provides the following narrative link:
'The people had grown weary. They had already spent many days travelling to the port, some by train, others on foot or on horseback or by cart. They had been asked to wait while the ship was being made ready. Finally, one of the ship's officers told them to come on board. He led them down many stairways and along dark passages until they came to their quarters in steerage.'

d   The teacher signals to the pupils to come and stand with him at the entrance to the square formed by the chairs. In role, he explains that this space will be their living quarters for the days to come. He tells them about the conditions under which they will be travelling, about meal times, exercise breaks, areas that are out of bounds etc. He warns them of the need to take great care of their belongings. The shipping company cannot be held responsible for any loss.

They are taken into 'steerage', told to find themselves an area that will be theirs for the rest of the journey and to settle themselves down by collecting bedding, carrying and stacking luggage and making a sleeping space. The ship's officer moves around checking identity cards and making a list of those present. He also checks on the luggage they have with them.

e   The passengers are asked to appoint two or three people who will be responsible for liaising with the ship's officer if there are any grievances. He will return shortly to hear who has been appointed and to deal with any matters that may have arisen in that time.

g It is important for the teacher to sit in with the group on this kind of exercise since individual pupils may need a great deal of supportive comment and questioning. Seemingly anachronistic offerings must be accepted for the moment since it is the associations which the object engenders which are important rather than its exact description.

h The teacher now deals with the complaints of each emigrant directly, since his earlier attempt at encouraging the group to elect representatives for this purpose proved inappropriate.

The officer uses this opportunity to paint a very grim picture of conditions on board. Few of the complaints can be dealt with. It is regrettable but they must remember that as steerage passengers they have paid very little for their passage and must really count themselves fortunate to be on the ship at all. Things will be much worse when they arrive in America since entry regulations are now very strict.

4a The non-verbal nature of this task should help to prevent characters and attitudes becoming too rigidly fixed at this early stage in the work.

c This activity may help to increase the level of commitment and reinforce the kind of attitudes appropriate to the situation.

f In pairs, each person tells their partner about the reasons why they have decided to travel to America. Members of family groups are split up so that they have a chance to work with 'strangers'.

The teacher invites some of the emigrants to share their story with the rest of the group.

g Each person has brought with them an object which may have little financial worth but is important to them for other reasons. That object is a direct link with their past life and has many associations with former days. Seated in a circle, the emigrants show the object (in mime) and explain why it is important.

h The pupils work as a whole group: the teacher readopts his role as ship's officer and comes into 'steerage' to ask if there are any problems. He wants the emigrants to present their grievances in an orderly way, and sets up a table in their quarters so that he can sit and write their names down as they came forward. The passengers present a long list of complains about the cramped conditions, poor food, lack of privacy, inadequate security and the generally squalid conditions in which they are forced to travel.

3   REFLECTION

Whole group

The teacher asks the group to list the words that could be used to describe the plight of the people they have been looking at in the drama. He writes these up on the blackboard and then asks the pupils to construct some sentences summing up the kind of experiences the travellers have been through.

Was the journey worth it, he asks. Perhaps it will help them find an answer to that question if they spend some time looking at the lives these people have left behind. This lesson has just been the starting-point for a drama about a group of people involved in a journey that will mean great changes for them.
[The topic was explored in a number of ways in later lessons.]

4   FURTHER DEVELOPMENTS

Looking at the past

a In groups of four or five, pupils create a series of tableaux showing aspects of the community from which these people have come. Those who have already been working in family groups can present a picture of that family at home or at work. Other groups might concentrate on showing members of the community engaged in a common task or occupation.

b The reason for leaving: the same groups prepare a short scene which shows the incident that finally makes these people decide to leave. The scenes can be used to provide additional information and perhaps lend further insights to the pupils' understanding of why such migration took place.

c In role as a neighbour or friend, the teacher joins each of the groups in turn and questions the individuals about their decision and their hopes for the future.

5*a*   This activity would be advisable only for those classes with some experience of movement work.

6   After 1898 newly-arrived immigrants were 'processed' at a vast reception centre on Ellis Island in New York harbour. There they were subjected to long periods of waiting while checks of various kinds were carried out. Those who managed to satisfy the immigration officials on all counts were taken by ferry to the mainland, some bearing new names given to them by people who could not understand the immigrant's native tongue. Undesirables were put back on board the ship that had brought them.

   A list of questions and procedures can be drawn up by the teacher before the lesson and given to those pupils who will represent the officials. The teacher will need to remain in overall charge of the activity, working perhaps in the role of one of the senior officials.

   The room can be set up to provide separate waiting areas and interview rooms with tables and chairs for the interviewers, though not necessarily for the immigrants who will be asked to stand. Signs and notices can be used to denote specific areas, especially that leading to the ferry quay where passengers board for New York.

7   From the 1880s patriotic organizations became increasingly opposed to the continuing immigration. By 1882 legislaton had been passed which refused entry to certain categories of people, namely those with known criminal records, the mentally ill and anyone likely to be a drain on public money. In the early years of the twentieth century political agitators were excluded, as were TB sufferers and epileptics. There was continued agitation for immigrants to be given a literacy test, but the proposals were never made law.

d   The teacher works in role as the agent of the shipping company and questions the would-be emigrants about their contacts in America, their financial resources and the kind of work they will be prepared to do if they get there.

5   ON BOARD SHIP

a   In movement, each person individually acts out a dream of the future in America.

b   In small groups the pupils show an incident which takes place on board. If possible these incidents should have wider implications and raise issues that may have consequences for the emigrants as a group. For example, if there is sickness on board will the passengers be turned away when they reach New York? Is it best to conceal illness not only for the sake of the family concerned but for the good of all who travel with them?

6   ARRIVAL AT ELLIS ISLAND

The teacher works in role with the help of some aides (other pupils, older pupils, teachers). They represent immigration officials working at the reception centre on Ellis Island. They project a harassed and unsympathetic attitude, moving people around from one interview to another, denying their requests for information and separating the members of family groups. They carry out health checks (in question form only), examine identify cards and make a long series of enquiries about political views, previous occupations, job prospects in America, the amount of dollars they have to keep them going, whether they have any relatives who would be willing to look after them etc. Particular problems can be fed in at the discretion of the teacher. Some people may be turned away or separated from their friends just as they are about to board the ferry to New York. No reason need be given for the detention. Some people may be put back on board ship; perhaps they are suspected of being political undesirables or a possible health risk and, therefore, a drain on the public funds.

7   IN AMERICA

a   In pairs, a newly-arrived immigrant meets a friend or relative who has been in the country for some years. What advice is the newcomer given? The roles are subsequently reversed so that each pupil has the opportunity to represent their original character.

b   The new immigrants apply for jobs. The interviews are carried out either with the pupils working in small groups, some of them taking on the employer's role, or they can be carried out by the teacher in that role with the whole group representing a large number of people who have come to apply for only a limited number of vacancies.

Written tasks

A letter from a relation or friend already in America.

A letter to the shipping company.

A very factual description of the community they come from, written as for a geography or history textbook.

A report in the local newspaper.

A map of the district from which they came.

A picture of their home.

A picture of the object they have brought with them.

A poem on their dream of the future.

A newspaper report of the incident on board ship, which is very biased against the immigrants.

A section of the ship's log.

A diary of the voyage.

A medical report for the Authorities on the health of the immigrants.

A report from the agents to the shipping company.

An advertisement for the shipping company.

A letter home.

A list of instructions for arrivals at Ellis Island.

Applications for jobs.

A personal memoir.

How difficult is it to get work? In small groups, pupils show what happens to those who fail to gain employment in spite of the prospects held out to them in the Old World.

  c In small groups, they show some of the other difficulties faced by the new arrivals. Do they meet with any prejudice? How easy is it for them to find accommodation? Are they exploited in any way? What help do they get and from whom? Are their expectations borne out by the reality of the situation?

8   ESTABLISHED MEMBERS OF THE COMMUNITY
  a People who were on the boat together meet again after a number of years. This can be set up as a whole-group activity with the teacher welcoming them all to a reunion, or the meeting could be shown as a series of small-group presentations. In the course of the reunion each person describes what life in America has been like for them.
  b In groups, pupils prepare a piece of movement which reflects the experience of the immigrants.

FURTHER READING
Cooke, Alistair, *America*, BBC Publications, 1973
Doctorow, E. L., *Ragtime*, Macmillan, 1976
Hartmann, Edward G., *American Immigration*, Minneapolis: Lerner Publications, 1979
Jones, Maldwyn A., *Destination America*, Weidenfeld & Nicolson, 1976

TEACHING NOTES

In order to fulfil these objectives the teacher had devised a structure that would offer pupils some clearly-defined tasks: in fact, a number of linked exercises and games used as part of the fictional context.

The authority of the 'Beowulf' role allows the teacher to operate from a position where he can retain some degree of control over a large and often unruly group.

The teacher is aware that the girls in this class will not easily identify with the kind of role this context imposes on them, but at this point he needs to have the pupils working as one group. He refers to them all as 'loyal followers' and tries to leave specific roles and responsibilities unstated.

I   This form of ritual may provoke some initial embarrassment for both teacher

12 *Legend*

INTRODUCTORY LESSON

This lesson took place with a first-year group in the drama room for a double period of seventy minutes.

Objectives
The pupils were accustomed to working in small groups and producing work that was highly action-oriented. The teacher wanted to introduce them to a format that would help to wean them away from this kind of activity but still provide them with a satisfying and productive experience.

Drama formed part of the first year integrated studies course. As part of that course they were currently reading the legend of Beowulf. The teacher explained that he was going to set up some work that would look at certain aspects of the story and the main events would be recalled in discussion.

Preparation
The teacher would like the pupils to adopt the roles of Beowulf's followers, those who go with him to meet the monster Grendel. He takes on the role of Beowulf. The pupils arrange their chairs in a circle. This represents Beowulf's hall. When the teacher asked how the followers would come to the hall, these pupils decided that they would arrive in pairs, be greeted by their lord and take their seat within the circle.

They move to a corner of the room and the teacher announces: 'Beowulf summons his loyal companions.'

1 THE REUNION

Whole group
Beowulf's people arrive at the hall. When they are all present he bids them

and pupils but it can help to encourage each individual's response to the make-believe, albeit in a very limited way. It may also help to signal appropriate serious-ness and behaviour. On this occasion there were many giggles before the strange-ness of the experience gradually wore off and the exercise created any sense of commitment. It will be important for the teacher to lend conviction to the formality of the ritual.

At this point in the drama the teacher does not want to give the pupils the chance to say 'no' to the prospect of the adventure that lies ahead. For the moment he is concerned to create a sense of group identity — in terms of both the actual and fictional contexts. If someone subsequently refuses to go through with the plan then this will open up an interesting line of development. What are the ties that bind these people to this one man and to each other? What are the responsibilities of the individual to the group? What punishments await those who refuse to be bound by the oath of loyalty?

There is no shortage of pupils willing to volunteer. Where individuals fail to remove the stick without being identified by its 'guardian', the teacher excuses their failure by recognizing that a task such as this can sometimes prove extremely difficult to accomplish in spite of the care taken.

[There was intense absorption from all concerned throughout this long section.]

b   The teacher encourages the story-tellers by offering comments which sup-port their contributions: 'Of course . . . I remember now. That was indeed a great time for us.' He occasionally feigns forgetfulness of the event in order to encourage welcome and reminds them that it has been a long time since their last gathering. Can anyone still remember the oath they made each other on that occasion? One of the companions suggests that it was 'All for one and one for all'. Others add their agreement.

Moving round the circle, the teacher faces each pupil in turn and takes their hand in a special handshake. He asks each one to say the oath with him. When he has returned to his place they all repeat the oath in unison. He holds up a stick for all to see. This, Beowulf's stick, will be their standard.

He reaffirms his pleasure at once again seeing so many of his loyal friends. He has called them here to listen to his news. He tells them of a tale he has heard, of how a monster called Grendel has killed many of Earl Hrothgar's people. Some of those present say that they too have heard this story and speak of what they know.

Beowulf says that he would like to set sail for Hrothgar's land and take up the fight against this monster. He knows that many of those now present will be eager to go with him on this adventure, but first of all he would like to present them with a challenge. Will they be prepared to undertake some tests which he has devised? He needs to be reminded once again of his companions' great skills. The tests are designed to illustrate those qualities which may be essential if the venture is to be a success.

2   THE TEST OF STEALTH

a   Grendel is a cunning monster. It may be necessary to set a trap for him. Stealth will prove to be a valuable asset; it has often been so in the past.

In role, the teacher places a chair in the centre of the circle. Under it he lays down a stick ('Beowulf's stick'). The test is quite simple. Whoever volunteers will be asked to remove the stick and take it back to his or her place without making a noise. Another member of the group will be sitting on the chair with eyes closed and will point in the direction of the slightest sound. The attempt fails if the volunteer is caught in the process of removing the stick.

The teacher adapts a fairly well-known game to serve his purposes here, generally known as 'Keeper of the Keys'. (In its traditional form, a bunch of keys is placed under a chair in the centre of a large circle. The 'keeper' sits on the chair and is blindfolded. A volunteer tries to retrieve the keys without being caught out and, if successful, becomes the new 'keeper'.) Since the teacher has already used a stick as a sign of Beowulf's authority he decides to give this additional prominence by making it the object to be retrieved from beneath the chair. The person from whom it has to be taken becomes the 'guardian' of the stick. The teacher occasionally provides a commentary which anticipates the kind of adventures in which the followers may become involved: 'Our standard has fallen into enemy hands but the one who guards it now lies asleep. It will take an act of stealth and courage to rescue it. See how well our companions perform this undertaking.'

b   At intervals during the course of this activity, Beowulf asks whether any of those present can recall previous occasions when this kind of stealth proved invaluable.

an extended contribution from the story-teller. 'My memory has failed me. Say how it was we escaped from the trap.'

   c Both this activity and the preceding one do not remain isolated exercises but are an integral part of the action. Not only do they provide links between the various attempts to retrieve the stick but they also help to lend the whole event an appropriate sense of occasion. The pupils' verbal contributions are often very vivid, their language entirely in keeping with the situation.

3   This may prove to be a difficult moment for the teacher since the task lacks both the carefully defined rules of the first test and its element of excitement. The content may be embarrassing so the teacher must be ready to intervene if the volunteers seem to be in trouble or exposed to the observers' critical comments. On this particular occasion the pupils were able to sustain the drama with sensitivity and with the same degree of concern they had exhibited throughout the lesson.

4   There were no giggles this time. Each pupil was prepared to contribute without any sign of reticence or embarrassment.

5   The pupils covered aspects of this work in their next English lesson. They drew

The companions tell of those times when their ability to move quietly and surely has helped to save their own and others' lives.

c The teacher also uses the activity to initiate a vocabulary-building exercise. As Beowulf, he muses aloud how best to describe the nature of the quietness he seeks. The pupils offer a long catalogue of similes. Beowulf praises their skill with words.

3 THE TEST OF CONCERN

Beowulf's followers will need many kinds of qualities. When people do not return from a dangerous undertaking, the news of their death has to be broken to a relative in an appropriate, sympathetic way.

The teacher (in role) says that this may be a harder test than the first. It requires a different kind of courage. He would like to see how his companions tell parents that their child has failed to return from the adventure. He sets up a series of incidents within the circle in which pupils are invited to represent the characters in the kind of situations described. What is the best way to break the news? What comfort can the messenger bring? The observers offer advice as to how the situations might be replayed. Sometimes it is best if the news is given quickly; at other times it may be necessary to approach the task indirectly and wait for an opportune moment.

Volunteers come forward to take on the roles of mothers, fathers, relatives and family friends, though the teacher allows only two or three people to be involved in each situation.

Beowulf comments on the skill with which the task has been performed. It has been good to be reminded of his friends' talents.

4 THE ADVENTURE TO COME

Are there any questions the followers would now like to ask about the adventure to come? They may want to know how they will travel to Hrothgar's kingdom, how large the boats will be, what Grendel looks like, how they will best be able to trap him. The teacher refers to some of the questions to those present who possess greater knowledge of specific areas. For example, those who may know something of boat-building.

The discussion is brought to an end. The followers are asked to return in one week's time in order to prepare for the journey. Before they take their leave, Beowulf asks each person present to make the oath with which they began their meeting. They pass Beowulf's standard around the circle and hold it aloft as they speak the oath. He says that if he should die in battle, they must make sure the standard does not fall into enemy hands. The companions call out the oath in unison.

5 DISCUSSION

The teacher praises the pupils for their excellent contributions. He asks them why

plans of the ships that would take them to Hrothgar's land and designed the weapons they would need.

6b   There could be later additions to the frieze, illustrating the defeat of Grendel and his mother.

d   The teacher will need to appoint a 'Hrothgar', and possibly some important members of his household. With what formalities would the two parties meet?

e   The success of this exercise will rely heavily upon the teacher's ability to evoke an atmosphere of suspense. As the monster, he slowly moves towards the 'sleeping' companions, pauses and moves away again. The slightest sound or movement causes him to stop altogether or give up the attempt. The teacher's example may serve as a model for other 'Grendels'. Narration can also help to build atmosphere here.

they think this quest is important to Beowulf, why his followers were prepared to undergo the trials he had planned for them and what each person would gain by following their lord on this adventure.

In the next lesson they might need to spend some time looking at the kind of preparations needed before the journey could begin.

6 FURTHER DEVELOPMENTS

a In pairs, 'A' and 'B' exchange stories about the monster Grendel. The accounts may be grossly exaggerated, the result of unsubstantiated rumours.

b In small groups, the pupils prepare a frieze which represents in tableau form the plight of Hrothgar and the havoc wreaked on his people by the monster's. raids. The sections of the 'tapestry' could also be drawn.

c In pairs, one of Beowulf's companions explains to an unsympathetic relative just why the venture is so important. What does each individual hope to gain from it? Why are the followers prepared to put their lives at risk? Do they have the option of not supporting Beowulf in this quest?

d Beowulf's followers come to Hrothgar's hall. They try to convince him (and his people) of their great skill and of their suitability for the task in hand. He may require proof. How do they demonstrate their talent without offending Hrothgar who has so far failed to outwit the monster?

e Beowulf sets up a practice situation to show his followers the way in which Grendel is to be caught. The monster will be lured to the hall by their feigned sleep. The slightest move may cause him to retreat before Beowulf can get close enough to attack. Beowulf himself will become the monster, creeping slowly and quietly toward the hall. He appoints one of his companions to represent himself for the purposes of the trial. Only if the whole group can manage to lure the monster to a certain place in the room will it be safe for the 'Beowulf' to attack (in ritualized, slow-motion movement). The responsibility for the success of the plan depends, therefore, on the ability of his followers to remain silent and motionless until they have got their adversary where they want him.

Alternative versions using different individuals can be tried out in action.

f In small groups, pupils enact the events of the night when Grendel was defeated. The events are shown in slow motion, without words, the hazily recalled memories of a confusing occasion. The scenes could be accompanied by a sound collage made by members of the group not involved in the action and either played back on tape or performed live.

g The followers recount the story of their success as part of a celebratory gathering. Different groups can make up their own retelling of the story or it can be done as a whole group exercise with the pupils seated in a circle and adding one word or one sentence to the corporate retelling.

h In pairs, the companions talk to a twentieth-century interviewer and describe the events of that period. They explain why they undertook the adventure, why they were prepared to risk so much and why they owed such loyalty to one man. What were his responsibilities to them?

TEACHING NOTES

In this particular class, the boys were the leaders, and were more articulate and active in drama than the girls who were prepared to go along with the boys' ideas.

1   For the first part of the lesson, the class was working at the level of dramatic play, relying heavily for ideas and vocabulary on TV and film representations of space travel. They reproduced appropriate language and attitudes with considerable skill.

13 *Starship*

INTRODUCTORY LESSON

This was a lesson with a fourth-year class in a drama studio in a double period.

Objective
The teacher's aim was to help the class to confront the notion of sexual stereo-typing. Using drama to approach the issue presented the class with an unexpected situation to which they had to respond, and an unusual point of view.

Preparation
The teacher, without any introductory discussion, asks the class to arrange the furniture in the studio to suggest the control-room of a starship. How can they best use the rostra blocks, tables and chairs which are available to them and create the control-room of a starship which will travel to the farthest galaxies?

1 THE LAUNCH

Working with considerable enthusiasm, the pupils set up a convincing 'bridge' and choose roles for themselves as captain, navigator, engineer, and so on. The teacher asks the crew to launch the ship on her journey to the stars. Led by one pupil, in this case the boy who has been chosen as captain, the class goes through a spontaneous 'take-off' procedure, and the starship is on its way.

The teacher reinforces what is happening by providing a narrative link for the first stages of the journey:
'The Starship *Orion* took off on the first stages of her mission of exploration, which would take her beyond the farthest galaxies to the edges of the universe. The crew watched as the familiar surface of the planet Earth rushed away beneath them, and was lost among the stars. No one knew what adventures lay ahead.'

During the next phase of the lesson, the class play at spaceships – the crew

2   The teacher's intervention puts an obstacle in the way of this 'playing' by the pupils, but it is sufficiently intriguing to gain their attention. If the teacher allows the 'dramatic play' to continue for too long, it becomes difficult to interrupt effectively.

For much of this lesson, the majority of the class observe the interaction of the captain and his henchmen with the Alien. They seem to feel themselves very much part of the drama, and are prepared to make suggestions and give advice where the opportunity arises.

3   The teacher was surprised by the rapidity with which the class recognized the implication of what the Alien was demanding – that the starship had come across a 'planet of women', as one boy called it. If the pupils had failed to realize what the Alien meant, the voice could have become more explanatory, or the teacher could have stopped the drama, and clarified what was happening in a brief discussion.

The girls seemed quite prepared to accept the captain's suggestion, and agreed very readily to deceive the Alien.

communicating with ground control and sending messages to other crew members. Soon, the engineers report a fault in the engine and this provides a topic for interaction and discussion.

2 THE VOICE

Suddenly, the teacher interrupts, speaking in a loud mechanical voice from the edge of the room: 'Contact. Contact. Come in please, Starship *Orion*.'

There is some confusion from the class, who hear the message, but are unsure how to respond. The teacher repeats: 'Contact. Contact. Starship *Orion*, you are in orbit round our planet. Please make contact.'

The communications officer, urged by the captain, replies: 'This is the Starship *Orion*. What do you want?'

Still speaking in a loud voice, the teacher answers: 'I wish to speak to the captain of your starship. Please put me in touch with your captain.'

The rest of the class are listening to these exchanges. The captain takes over from the communications officer and makes contact with the Alien voice: 'This is the captain of Starship *Orion*. What do you want?

The teacher, as the Alien voice, replies: 'I wish to talk to the captain of the starship.'

The boy who has taken the role of captain insists: 'I am the captain.'

The teacher replies: 'Impossible'.

The captain repeats that it is he who is speaking. The rest of the crew are now listening intently.

The teacher replies: 'It is impossible that you are the captain of the starship. Our sensors show that there are male and female creatures aboard your ship. It is impossible that your captain should be a male. I wish to speak to your captain.'

3 THE MEETING

This creates some confusion among the crew. At first, the captain tries to insist that he *is* the captain, but the Alien merely repeats 'Impossible'.

The crew rapidly realize the implications of what the Alien is saying, and hold a hurried discussion. Almost immediately, the captain decides that the medical officer, a girl, must pretend to be the captain. This girl accepts his decision passively, and comes forward to the bridge.

The Alien makes contact: 'Are you the captain of this starship?'

The girl confirms this. The Alien enquires who was speaking before, and the girl explains that it was the communications officer. The Alien replies : 'Impossible. Males are not sufficiently intelligent for such positions of responsibility.'

The girl is confused and her replies are prompted by the rest of the crew.

The class seemed fully prepared to accept any 'technology' possessed by the Alien, and did not question or reject her powers. The teacher had anticipated that one reaction might be to leave the planet and continue the journey to somewhere safer, but the class was prepared to work within the rules of the game. The pupils seemed to realize that it would be more interesting to confront the problem and try to solve it, rather than abandon the situation and 'escape'. Their acceptance of the teacher's intervention may have been helped by the pattern of such TV programmes as 'Star Trek', in which the crew of the starship are regularly confronted by unexpected problems.

If the class do decide to 'escape', it may still be possible at a later stage to pick up the problem again, either in discussion or enactment. For example, groups could show what had happened to previous starships which had ventured into the orbit of this planet, or could prepare scenes which would show what life on the alien planet might be like.

4   The attitude of the Alien is now completely different. She appears very friendly and welcoming, but refuses to take the boys seriously, and is very patronizing towards them. They find it difficult to cope with this, but in spite of their frustration, maintain their roles with great seriousness. [The lesson ended with the teacher narrating the departure of the starship *Orion* from the planet, where they were forced to leave their captain and several of the crew behind them.]

During this lesson, the boys were confronted with unexpected attitudes and were forced to rethink their belief in their position. The girls remained largely passive during the lesson, accepting the boys' decisions, which reflected the actual class dynamics. Their attitudes during the drama provided an interesting basis for later discussion which was at first about the events of the drama, and whether the crew of the starship had made the right decisions. Later the discussion broadened to cover sexual stereotyping and the role of women in society.

5   **FURTHER DEVELOPMENTS**

   a   In pairs: explaining to a parent or friend that one is about to follow a career or make a decision which will go counter to usually accepted sex roles.

   b   In small groups: scenes which show the kinds of discrimination which women have faced in the past.

   c   In pairs: talk to a friend of the opposite sex, and try to discover what is their view of the position of women.

   d   Preparing scenes to prove to the Alien that men and women have equal rights and opportunities on the planet Earth; preparing scenes to explain how the Alien planet came to adopt this extreme view of the roles of the sexes.

   e   Whole group: a tribunal in which the class challenges the attitudes of the Alien and brings evidence which proves that men deserve to be treated equally.

The Alien requests that the captain and the chief officers of the starship should land on the surface of the planet. The captain picks other girls to accompany the girl who is pretending to be captain. They are 'beamed down' to the planet.

The girls move away from the 'starship' as the rest of the class watches. They are met by the Alien, who asks them if they are telling the truth. The girls insist that they are. The Alien says that she has a scanner which can read their memories and which will determine whether they have been telling the truth. After a few moments, she announces that they have been giving her false information. Why have they been lying? The girls are lost for an answer.

The Alien is not angry, but cannot understand the reason for this deception. She explains that their starship is now held in orbit around the planet by a force-field, and cannot escape without the agreement of the aliens. She sends the girl and her companions back to the starship.

4 THE CAPTAIN'S VISIT

They are eagerly questioned by the other members of the crew, and the captain holds a formal discussion in order to decide what should be done. At last, it is agreed that the captain and the most important members of his crew should descend to the surface of the planet and try to convince the Alien that they are capable of intelligent thought. The captain makes contact with the Alien voice and requests permission to land on the planet. The Alien agrees.

As soon as the captain and his three companions leave the starship they are greeted warmly by the Alien. This lack of hostility disconcerts them. She welcomes them to the planet and offers to provide them with anything they may require for their comfort and well-being. The captain states the purpose of his visit in dignified tones – he wishes to convince her that men can be intelligent, and explains that on the planet Earth men and women are equal. The Alien waves his explanation aside. There are only two reasons for the continued existence of men on her planet, she explains. These are to be part of the breeding programme and to assist with heavy construction work. She compliments the crew members on being fine physical specimens and says that she is sure that they will prove very valuable. The boys demand to be allowed back to the starship, but the Alien refuses. She says she will release the starship from orbit round the planet but will keep the captain and his companions. The captain accepts this with dignity, but warns the Alien that she will not get away with this, and that Starfleet will return to rescue them.

TEACHING NOTES

1   Pupils will need to accept the anachronism of radio at this period in history.
   They may lack confidence at first in their knowledge of the play. It will be important to stress that the people they choose to be will only have a partial knowledge of what has been happening in the castle. They may be misinformed about some events, or have seen only some of what has happened so that they may make mistakes. The interviewers must be encouraged to accept what they hear and to be positive in their questioning. It may be possible to record the interviews if equipment is available.

2   This exercise requires the pupils to understand the structure of the play, so that they can select significant moments. Each group could prepare one picture, or select five or six important moments in the play. Some groups may wish to make rough sketches of the 'pictures' before enacting them. The other groups can be asked to provide titles for each picture after they have watched them.

14 *Macbeth*

INTRODUCTORY LESSON

This lesson took place with a class of fourth years in a classroom for a double period. The class had been studying *Macbeth* as an examination text.

Objectives
The objective for the lesson was to use drama strategies to diagnose the extent of the pupils' knowledge of the play, to reinforce that knowledge and to motivate them to a further close study of the text.

Preparation
The teacher asks the class to recall briefly the events at the end of the play, when Macbeth is defeated and Malcolm and his followers have captured Dunsinane.

1 AN OUTSIDE BROADCAST

In pairs
'A' is a member of a team which is preparing a radio broadcast about the fall of Macbeth. 'A' is engaged in preliminary research for the programme, and 'B', the partner, is someone whom they have chosen to interview, and who may be useful in the programme. 'B' has been associated in some way with the events of the play, perhaps as a servant in Dunsinane, a former follower of Macbeth, a peasant from the countryside round the castle, or one of the soldiers in Malcolm's victorious army. What inside information can the interviewer obtain from 'B'.

2 KEY MOMENTS

Small groups
Working in small groups, the class prepare 'pictures' of vital incidents in Macbeth's career. These are the kind of pictures which might accompany an illustrated edition of the text, or be used as 'stills' to advertise a film of the play.

3   In this pair work it will be important to stress that these are fictional incidents, invented so that certain scenes in the play can be examined in a different way. They do not occur in the text!

It may be useful for the class to look at relevant scenes before tackling these exercises, or to recall details in discussion. What are the arguments which Lady Macbeth and Macduff use to persuade Macbeth and Malcolm, in their respective scenes? Was Macduff wise to go to England?

It may be appropriate to eavesdrop on some of these scenes, or to ask some of the pairs to repeat their conversation, so that the rest of the class can hear the kinds of arguments they are using.

4   In this particular lesson, Lady Macbeth's sister was played by another member of the English department, but it is not necessary to have someone actually present in this role. The teacher may have been requested to hold such a tribunal by the new regime, or may have received a letter from the sister.

Because each group is required to examine only a single scene, it should be possible to produce precise evidence in a short space of time.

3   EXTENSIONS

In pairs
  a   The pupils are asked to imagine that Banquo has a wife who is just as ambitious for him as Lady Macbeth is for her husband. How does she react when Banquo tells her about the witches' prophecy to him? What arguments does she use? Are they the same as those used by Lady Macbeth to influence Macbeth?
  b   Macduff has decided to go to England. He confides his decision to a friend. His friend is not sure that he is doing the right thing, and tries to dissuade him.
  c   One partner is Malcolm, at the court of King Edward. The other is a spy sent by Macbeth to lure Malcolm back to Scotland. What kinds of persuasion does he use?

4   THE TRIBUNAL

a   *Whole group*
The teacher introduces a colleague in role as Lady Macbeth's sister, who refuses to believe that Lady Macbeth is the 'fiend-like queen' she is thought to be and demands that a tribunal be set up to enquire into her guilt.

b   *Small groups*
In groups of three or four, the pupils are asked to consider one scene in which Lady Macbeth appears. What evidence can each group find from their single scene to prove her guilty or innocent?
  The tribunal is set up and each group gives evidence in turn, using only the information in the scene they have been looking at. Someone in each group explains how they came by their information – perhaps they overheard the conversations between Lady Macbeth and her husband, or they were a guest at the banquet, a servant in the castle, or a nurse or doctor.
  Lady Macbeth's sister refuses to believe the evidence. She admits that her sister was very loyal to her husband and likely to have been influenced by him, but will not believe that she was evil. Some of the class agree with her and others do not. A vote is taken to decide the verdict, but Lady Macbeth's sister intends to make further enquiries.

5   FURTHER DEVELOPMENTS

  a   A series of news bulletins describing the political changes which occur in the play. It may be that they have to be presented so as not to give offence.
  b   Lady Macbeth's eldest child tells a younger sister or brother what has happened to their parents.
  c   Malcolm is interviewed at a later stage in his reign.
  d   Finding modern analogies for the story of Macbeth.
  e   Putting the witches on trial for their part in the tragedy.

TEACHING NOTES

None of the pupils had ever been destructive or refused to participate but some of them had found it difficult to adopt and maintain a role without an obvious sense of embarrassment. They were co-operative but lacking in confidence.

Though the class is not particularly familiar with this strategy, the teacher is anxious to provide them with a framework for drama which allows them all to start from the same point and work towards a common goal, though by different methods. In his planning, he has decided that a role will allow him to initiate the drama in this way and will also enable him to intervene later in an organizational capacity.

1*a*   The lay-out of the room has been arranged by the teacher before the pupils arrive: they sit at tables arranged in a circle. This may help to encourage a sense of security — for the moment, at least, they will not be asked to stand and act!

15 Advertising Campaign

This lesson took place with a fourth-year group working in a classroom for a double period of seventy minutes.

Objectives
The class had very limited experience of drama. On previous occasions some pupils had been happy to involve themselves in the activity but others were reluctant to participate. The teacher's current concern was to devise a framework that would allow both groups to commit themselves in their own way and at their own pace and still have an equal stake in the development and outcomes of the drama.

Preparation
The teacher explains that the work he has planned will provide an opportunity for the pupils to choose from a variety of roles and activities. Although he intends to start the drama with the class working as one large group, they will subsequently be able to split up into small groups according to their particular interests. He tells them that he will work in role for the first activity and asks them to represent a group of people, a team, who work for an advertising company. In order to be able to give them further instructions and to get the drama started quickly, he will now begin to speak to them in role as the co-ordinator of that team.

1 INTRODUCING THE CAMPAIGN

a *Whole group*
The teacher makes an opening announcement:
'Here at . . . we've had a very successful year. No one has been more successful than the members of the particular team who are now sitting at these tables.

The pupils are designated 'experts' in a particular field. This means that the teacher will have to accept their expertise. Factual inconsistencies can be set straight afterwards but for the sake of the drama the teacher must, for the moment, take what the pupils give him. His role will allow him to ask questions or make recommendations which help pupils to develop what may initially seem to be a superficial line of thought and action.

The teacher lists some of the activities that might capture the interest of the group. The pupils suggest others. The range and nature of the activities may not accurately reflect the work of an actual advertising agency but they will be legitimate for *this* one. Any similarities and differences that exist between the two can be checked out later. For the moment it is important that the teacher accepts those suggestions that help to build the fictional context.

b   The teacher could have carried out this organizational task in role but the pupils' slow response leads him to work in a way with which they seem more at ease. The role can be readopted later if necessary.

c   The purpose of this strategy is to get an initial commitment from all the pupils. This particular activity should not pose too great a threat to the more reticent pupils. Though one of the teacher's concerns will be to get the group thinking and talking as if they were members of a team of specialists, he is content to move very slowly and win that kind of identification out of their growing interest in the task.

Congratulations! I've just been given another project for us to handle. I thought you would like to know about it straight away.'

The pupils are told that they are being made responsible for planning and preparing a television campaign to launch a new product. The teacher momentarily comes out of role to ask them if they would like to choose the nature of this product. This class decided that it should be a brand of cereal.

The co-ordinator resumes his introductory statement: 'We have very little time in which to get this campaign under way. The purpose of this meeting is simply to let you know the situation, get some ideas going and then you can go off and work on your particular part of the project. This team (our team) includes people who know something about performing in commercials, about writing scripts, designing sets and costumes. I know that some of you can advise us about the technical aspects of the filming, about camera angles and such like. There are others who can do the art-work. I'd like us to try out some ideas together here this afternoon before the campaign goes any further. So . . . any questions?'

The pupils ask if they can choose which task they want to do, whether they can work with friends and whether they need 'to do any acting'. The teacher tells them they can select any of the areas he has outlined in his opening statement and that they don't have to be involved in performing the commercial if they don't want to be. There are plenty of other things that need to be done. Of course they can work with friends: 'that seems to have produced good results for us so far'.

b *Selection*
The teacher comes out of role to check that everyone understands the situation. Most pupils say that they do. Some just nod an agreement. He spreads some sheets of paper on the table in front of him, and says that he will head each one with the title of the activity they would like to be involved in.
[These pupils chose to work in groups on:

— performing the commercials (3 groups)
— designing captions (2 groups)
— designing sets
— filming]

c *Small groups*
The teacher passes round four sheets bearing these headings and the pupils add their names to the respective lists.
He begins to discuss with them:

— the name of the product
— the selling angle they will use and the market they are aiming for
— the kind of dramatic situations that would be most effective
— the type of captions that will be used to accompany the action

2   This phase of the work requires a high degree of organization. The teacher must ensure that each group is fully aware of its tasks and be able to offer them advice, comment and encouragement. Some materials should be made available in advance. For this first lesson, paper, crayons, scissors etc. will probably be sufficient since the teacher can remind pupils that things are 'only at the planning stage'. If the set designers subsequently wish to construct a model of their sets, additional material can be made available later.

3   The teacher's role invites an in-role response from the pupils. The designers explain and justify their decisions as the people in the team who know something about the design. The teacher defers to their expertise and, as the person who doesn't really know very much about their specialism, he can also ask questions which challenge them to more detailed and sometimes more considered responses. The children now appear to accept the teacher in role much more readily than at first.

It is important for the teacher to spend time listening to the contributions of the pupils who will not be involved in presenting the commercials. He is concerned to bolster their confidence by giving due recognition to the contributions they have made to the collective effort.

4a   Since the client is present only in the person of the team co-ordinator, it allows him to ask for situations to be replayed if he feels they would not meet with this visitor's approval. For example, 'I wonder if he's going to be satisfied with what we've just shown him? Do you think there's another approach we could take that

2 PREPARING THE CAMPAIGN

Small groups

The groups disperse to begin work on their particular activity. Those responsible for performing the commercial agree on the basic situation each will present.

During the initial phase of their discussions they are joined by the pupils who have opted to work on set design. The members of the film crew attach themselves to two of the groups. They do not contribute much to the discussion. The teacher provides them with pencils and paper so that they can take notes and work out their camera angles. Those responsible for designing the visual captions work at tables moved to one corner of the room. They have been supplied with large pieces of card and felt-tip pens.

The teacher moves amongst the groups, half in/half out of role. As teacher, he deals with practical problems related to working space, materials etc., but as the team co-ordinator he frequently reminds groups of the good work they have come up with in past campaigns. He tells them that he feels the project to be in expert hands.

The set designers remove themselves from the group who will do the performing and begin to sketch out their plans of how the finished sets will look. They share the tables with the other designers.

3 REVIEWING THE PROGRESS OF THE CAMPAIGN

Whole group

The teacher calls all the groups together around the tables. He talks to them in role and first of all asks the set and caption designers to share their plans with the rest of the team. He wants to know the thinking behind their proposals. *Why* have they decided to approach a particular problem in this way? Did they consider alternative solutions?

He thinks the ideas might work well and praises them for their efforts. He asks the camera crew to talk about any problems they may have and wants to know how and when display material will be incorporated into the commercial?

During the course of this discussion there are occasional signs of unrest from those pupils who are waiting to perform their prepared scenes. The co-ordinator apologizes for the delay and explains that it is important for everyone to have a clear idea of the work in hand. He spends some time questioning the design groups and film crew and comments on their valuable offerings.

4 IMPRESSING THE CLIENT

a *Whole group*

The 'actors' prepare to show their work. Each of the three groups sets up their scene in a different part of the room. The teacher asks the observers to get into a position where they can see what is happening. He then tells them that as the team co-ordinator he will 'pretend to be an important official from the company whose

would be just that bit more effective? We have to convince someone very important that we know what we're doing. Try it again a different way. I'll pretend to be
the client one more time.'

Pupils generally have few problems in accepting the teacher in a number of
different roles or in a double role like this one, providing that each role is signalled
clearly enough.

The teacher is taking a considerable risk in delaying, yet again, the showing of the
scenes, but he uses the opportunity presented by his visitor's role to reinforce the
work of the other groups. The teacher may become pressed for time, but he must
allow each of the groups to present their scene before the lesson ends.

The teacher can employ this strategy to help the group operate more effectively
in theatre form.

5b   The purpose of this strategy would be to put the more reticent members of
the class into a more active, critical role. The situation should be set up formally.
The viewers are invited to the studio, sit in special seats and perhaps fill in
questionnaires. The teacher functions as co-ordinator of the event and, if necessary, as discussion leader.

product is being advertised'. He wants to see how the team could impress such a visitor with their expertise. Could they make a good job of selling their product to *this* potential buyer?

He walks to a corner of the room, puts on his jacket and announces himself as the client. He understands that the co-ordinator with whom he normally deals is not present but that the team is ready to show the results of their initial planning. The pupils welcome him, ask him to take a seat and, in response to his questions, explain that they will present some scenes for his viewing.

The visitor asks if there is anything to help him envisage what the sets and captions will look like. He has a poor imagination where these things are concerned. The designers and film crew give a *brief* summary of the results of their work and show him their plans.

b *Appraisal*

Members of the camera crew attach themselves to the two groups with whom they have previously been involved. They move around 'filming'.

At the end of each scene the client thanks the actors for their efforts and asks questions about why they have chosen to represent the situations in the ways they have done. He seems thoughtful, not particularly enthusiastic: the scenes lack shape and are over-long. As the lesson finishes he says that he will send them a list of comments which they might find useful. He thanks them for an interesting afternoon. There is a brief final discussion which is principally concerned with the kind of improvements that may be necessary if the agency is to mount a successful campaign.

5   FURTHER DEVELOPMENTS

   a   Using the list of visitor's comments as a guide, the performers revise their work. The visitor will be coming back soon to see what changes have been made.

The other pupils may want to develop interests arising out of the initial lesson or pursue new ones related to the topic. For example, composing 'jingles', preparing newspaper advertisements to accompany the television campaign etc.

   b   The finished commercials are shown to a viewing panel. The pupils not involved in performance are asked to adopt the roles of members of the public who have been co-opted on to these panels. Their task is to consider the effectiveness of each contribution and make recommendations if they feel these to be necessary.

   c   The class prepare a television programme about an advertising agency. In small groups, the pupils devise a number of scenes which show the respective departments at work. The scenes are linked together by a 'voice-over' commentary and each group can elect a narrator to point out important features of their particular expertise. For example, the designers enact the kind of discussion they might have when the work is in the early stages of planning, the actors show a part of the rehearsal process etc.

BIBLIOGRAPHY ON ADVERTISING

Heath, R. B., *The Persuaders*, Nelson, 1975
McShane, Dennis, *Using the Media*, Pluto Press, 1979
Rudinger, Edith, and Kelly, Vic, *Break for Commercials*, Connexions, Penguin, 1969
Thom, Vivien, *Advertising*, Edward Arnold, 1980
Williams, Alma, *Your Choice?*, Longman, 1980

USEFUL ADDRESSES

Advertising Standards Authority
15–17 Ridgemount Street
London WC1E 7AW

Advertising Association
Abford House
15 Wilton Road
London SW1V 1NJ

Affirm (Campaign against female stereotypes in advertising)
Women's Arts Alliance
10 Cambridge Terrace Mews
London NW1

d   The class prepare an investigative report on the nature and purpose of advertising. Where does the money come from to finance costly campaigns? What are the most effective forms of advertising? How do advertisements achieve their purpose?

The report consists of a series of interviews with members of the public, with clients and shopkeepers, with actors who appear in commercials etc. Pupils might also be encouraged to do some research on the advertising industry and present their findings as a series of informative statements or as small-group presentations.

e   In small groups, the class prepare a dual version of the same situation first as it might appear in reality, then as it might be represented in a television commercial. What differences are there between the two? Which aspects become distorted and why?

Select Bibliography

SELECT BIBLIOGRAPHY

Allen, John, *Drama in Schools: its theory and practice*, Heinemann, 1979
Bolton, Gavin, *Towards a Theory of Drama in Education*, Longman, 1979
Day, Christopher, *Drama in the Upper and Middle School*, Batsford, 1975
Dewey, John, *Experience and Education*, Collier Books, 1938
Esslin, Martin, *An Anatomy of Drama*, Maurice Temple Smith, 1976, Abacus edition, 1978
Fines, John, and Verrier, Ray, *The Drama of History*, New University Press, 1974
Gulbenkian Report: The Arts in Schools, Calouste, Gulbenkian Foundation, 1982
Jackson, Tony, (Editor), *Learning Through Theatre*, Manchester University Press, 1980
Johnson, Liz and O'Neill, Cecily, *Selected Writings of Dorothy Heathcote*, Hutchinson, 1983
Langer, Suzanne, *Feeling and Form: a theory of art*, Routledge and Keegan Paul, 1953
McGregor, Lyn; Robinson, Ken; and Tate, Maggie, *Learning Through Drama*, Heinemann, 1977
O'Neill, Cecily; Lambert, Alan; Linnell, Rosemary; Warr-Wood, Janet, *Drama Guidelines*, Heinemann, 1976
Robinson, Ken, (Editor), *Exploring Theatre and Education*, Heinemann, 1980
Stabler, Tom, *Drama in Primary Schools*, Macmillan, 1979
Stephenson, Norman, and Vincent, Denis, (Editors), *Teaching and Understanding Drama*, NFER Publishing Company, 1975
Wagner, Betty J., *Dorothy Heathcote: Drama as a Learning Medium*, Hutchinson, 1976

Index.